ALSO BY DIANE WAKOSKI

Coins & Coffins (1962)
Four Young Lady Poets (1962)
Discrepancies and Apparitions (1966)
The George Washington Poems (1967)
Greed: Parts 1 & 2 (1968)
The Diamond Merchant (1968)
Inside the Blood Factory (1968)
Thanking My Mother for Piano Lessons (1969)
The Lament of the Lady Bank Dick (1969)
Greed: Parts 3 & 4 (1969)
The Moon Has a Complicated Geography (1969)
Black Dream Ditty (1970)
The Magellanic Clouds (1970)
Greed: Parts 5-7 (1971)
On Barbara's Shore (1971)
The Motorcycle Betrayal Poems (1971)
Form Is an Extension of Content (1972)
Smudging (1972)
The Pumpkin Pie (1972)
Greed: Parts 8, 9 & 11 (1973)
Dancing on the Grave of a Son of a Bitch (1973)
Looking for the King of Spain (1974)
Trilogy: Coins & Coffins, Discrepancies and Apparitions,
    The George Washington Poems (1974)
The Fable of the Lion and the Scorpion (1975)
Creating a Personal Mythology (1975)
The Wandering Tattler (1975)
Virtuoso Literature for Two and Four Hands (1975)
Variations on a Theme (1976)
Waiting for the King of Spain (1976)
Pachelbel's Canon (1978)
The Man Who Shook Hands (1978)
Trophies (1979)
Cap of Darkness (1980)
The Magician's Feastletters (1982)
The Collected Greed, Parts 1-13 (1984)
Why My Mother Likes Liberace (1985)
The Rings of Saturn (1986)
Roses (1987)

DIANE WAKOSKI

EMERALD ICE

SELECTED POEMS 1962-1987

BLACK SPARROW PRESS / SANTA ROSA / 1988

ACKNOWLEDGEMENTS

The poems in this book are drawn from the following collections: *Coins & Coffins,* Hawk's Well Press, 1962; *Discrepancies and Apparitions,* Doubleday, 1966; *The George Washington Poems,* Riverrun Press, 1967; *Inside the Blood Factory,* Doubleday, 1968; *The Magellanic Clouds,* Black Sparrow Press, 1970; *The Motorcycle Betrayal Poems,* Simon & Schuster, 1971; *Smudging,* Black Sparrow Press, 1972; *Dancing on the Grave of a Son of a Bitch,* Black Sparrow Press, 1973; from *Looking for the King of Spain,* Black Sparrow Press, 1974; *Virtuoso Literature for Two and Four Hands,* Doubleday, 1975; *Waiting for the King of Spain,* Black Sparrow Press, 1976; *The Man Who Shook Hands,* Doubleday, 1978; *Cap of Darkness,* Black Sparrow Press, 1980; *The Magician's Feastletters,* Black Sparrow Press, 1982; *The Rings of Saturn,* Black Sparrow Press, 1986. "Emerald Ice" was published in *Sulfur* magazine. My thanks to the editors and publishers.

This project is funded in part by the California Arts Council, a State Agency.

LIBRARY OF CONGRESS CATALOGING-IN-PUBLICATION DATA

Wakoski, Diane, 1937
  Emerald ice: selected poems, 1962-1987.
    p.   cm.
ISBN 0-87685-745-4 :   ISBN 0-87685-746-2 (signed) :
    ISBN 0-87685-744-6 (pbk.) :
  I. Title.
PS3573.A42E4   1988
811'.54—dc19   88-25080
                                                    CIP

Emerald Ice

If I were a jeweler,
I'd look for emeralds the color of
healthy basil leaves, pungent and thick and green
as parrots;
and if I were a woman who had emeralds weighing down
her harpsichordian hands and nudging her neck
as they turn warm but do not melt,
I would hold my emerald-laden hand
against this new snow which covers the not yet frozen
November ground, the liquid hardness of the stones
contrasting with the chalky softness of the snow.
For just a moment at least until,
if I were an astronomer, mirroring an arc of light which
might mean a new galaxy
has been discovered, I might name
this phemonemon, "Emerald Ice,"
to tell you how
beautiful these things are to me.
But none of it would
matter, if I didn't dream of boys
with leather aviator jackets,
or men who rode motorcycles into the living room, once,
or the Silver Surfer who might travel with me,
nude of emeralds, a galactic wanderer.
What could matter
if there were any sex or love that could
transcend death,
speed faster than my imagination
or the light?
What could matter
if these boys,
if all men,
were not just memories like emeralds,
or pungent basil,
new snow,

11

The Few Silver Scales

The feeling comes,
the critics say, spontaneously. A gull
swooping to the water, grabbing food, and skill,
not contrived, but gracing
the dipping wings.
I know
what they say; have never
found it so.
How stiff my wings extend,
creaking like a boat
moored,
rocking in the waves.
And how
the morsel slips away
into the water,
sliding fish—only a few silver scales in my beak
after I dive to catch it.
The feeling comes,
lurching me, and I must grab it
as best I can.
How lucky I feel
with a few silver scales
dripping from my beak.

c. 1961

Justice Is Reason Enough

He, who once was my brother, is dead by his own hand.
Even now, years later, I see his thin form lying on the sand

where the sheltered sea washes against those cliffs
he chose to die from. Mother took me back there every day for
over a year and asked me, in her whining way, why it had to
     happen

over and over again — until I wanted
never to hear of David any more. How
could I tell her of his dream about the gull beating its wings
effortlessly together until they drew blood?

Would it explain anything, and how can I tell
anyone here about the great form and its beating wings. How it
swoops down and covers me, and the dark tension leaves

me with blood on my mouth and thighs. But it was that dream,
you must know, that brought my tight, sullen little

brother to my room that night and pushed his whole taut body
right over mine until I yielded, and together we yielded to the
     dark tension.
Over a thousand passing years, I will never forget
him, who was my brother, who is dead. Mother asked me why
every day for a year; and I told her justice. Justice is
reason enough for anything ugly. It balances the beauty in the
     world.

c. 1958

Elizabeth and the Golden Oranges

I

In packing boxes of spiders and amber,
under old letters, the stiff smell of folded satin
greets me tonight, in these quiet rooms:
a house dead, one that has never had life.
How proud my parents were of the wedding
pictures, their daughter in straight folds of silk —
if not beautiful, straight and clean: and the groom,
a man, that if they did not like, they had
to admire. How far all that is away.
The ink has turned brown; why do I open
these tall crates? So much unfulfilled time
has elapsed. My own hands are spiders
touching the satin, making webs from the box.

II

Zeno, with his arrows, saying they always
occupied a finite amount of space and proving
their static condition, disallowed progress
or change. He did not believe it. He saw
men live and die, not dying the same size
or in the same condition — baby-fine hair
turned to coarse hanks, milk coming from a cow's eating grass.
        He could not
believe, but wanted to know; arrows do not always reach
their targets. That is all I know. Not why
or how they get from one place to another.
The stiff smell of old satin greets me tonight.

III

Once married. Throw away twisted gold rings.
Cast them to the wind. Let spiders weave webs

about them, to glitter in the sun. Even a good
man would rather have a beautiful woman
than one who is not. She can stare in the mirror —
first lilies of the valley and April snow —
all day long and never turn a hand because
men love women who are beautiful, the bird
that flies out of an orange when you open
it. Who is the bird flying out of the orange
when you open it? There are so many birds.
The arrow does not progress, Zeno says;
but he sees the change in a man's hair.

IV

In packing boxes of spiders and amber,
you will never uncover the bone; the satin
is not stiff with blood but age. The arrow fell short.
There is bitterness in having only one chance
at your mark. Better to have never shot
at all. How often does a spider weave
a web? There is only one bird in every
orange. Leave gold rings at the circus.
Do not uncover the things you regret. My own
hands are spiders, crawling over this satin
handling letters that crackle like bones,
thinking of oranges from Spain
whose flesh is more fragrant than mine ever was.

c. 1957-58

Inside Out

I walk the purple carpet into your eye
carrying the silver butter server
but a truck rumbles by,
                    leaving its black tire prints on my foot
and old images   the sound of banging screen doors on hot
            afternoons and a fly buzzing over the Kool-Aid spilled on
            the sink
flicker, as reflections on the metal surface.

Come in, you said,
inside your paintings, inside the blood factory, inside the
old songs that line your hands, inside
eyes that change like a snowflake every second,
inside spinach leaves holding that one piece of gravel,
inside the whiskers of a cat,
inside your old hat, and most of all inside your mouth where you
grind the pigments with your teeth, painting
with a broken bottle on the floor, and painting
with an ostrich feather on the moon that rolls out of my mouth.

You cannot let me walk inside you too long inside
the veins where my small feet touch
bottom.
You must reach inside and pull me
like a silver bullet
from your arm.

c. 1964-65

Wind Secrets

I like the wind
with its puffed cheeks and closed eyes.
Nice wind.
I like its gentle sounds
and fierce bites.
When I was little
I used to sit by the black potbellied stove and stare
at a spot on the ceiling,
while the wind breathed and blew
outside.
"Nice wind,"
I murmured to myself.

I would ask mother when she kneeled to tie my shoes
what the wind said.

Mother knew.

And the wind whistled and roared outside
while the coals opened their eyes in anger
at me.
I would hear mother crying under the wind.
"Nice wind," I said,
But my heart leapt like a darting fish.
I remember the wind better than any sound.
It was the first thing I heard
with blazing ears,
a sound that didn't murmur and coo,
and the sounds wrapped round my head
and huffed open my eyes.
It was the first thing I heard
besides my father beating my mother.
The sounds slashed at my ears like scissors.
Nice wind.

Apparitions Are Not Singular Occurrences

When I rode the zebra past your door,
wearing nothing but my diamonds, I expected to hear bells
and see your face behind the thin curtins.
But instead I saw you, a bird, wearing the mask of a bird,
with all the curtains drawn, the lights blazing,
and Death drinking cocktails with you.
In your thin hand, like the claw of a bird, because you are a bird,
the drink reflected the light from my diamonds, passing by.

Your bird's foot, like thin black threads of bone or metal staples,
has the resistance necessary to keep death at a pleasant distance,
drinking his scotch and enjoying your company,
as he seldom has a chance; the zebra hide against my bare legs
is warm. The diamonds now warm on my neck,
on my fingers,
my feet,
my ears.
How Death looks at them
and my body
and the old man desires them all.

I rode by your windows, hoping you would see me and want me,
not knowing you already had a guest.
The diamonds I put on for you,
the clothes I took off,
and my zebra—did you see his eyes just slightly narrow
as we came by?
Not knowing Death would be there,
I rode by.
And Death and I see each other now so often
I have even thought of becoming a trapeze artist so that I might
swing on the bar away from him—so far up he'd never reach me,
but instead I see him more and more with all my friends,
drinking, talking,
and always keeping his elderly eyes on me.

And you, watching me ride by on my zebra and dressed
only in my diamonds,
were my one last hope.
But even you, wearing the mask of a bird, invited him to have
a drink and left the curtains drawn for him,
sharing something you had no right to share.

c. 1961

Follow That Stagecoach

The sense of disguise is a
rattlesnake and
it's easy to wake up and find it curled in your shoe.
Past Ghost Junction and Cody's Rock
the same stagecoach rattles day after day. Long days and short
    days
carrying the same passengers.
They keep away from you. Your six-shooter wanders into
hand, disguised
yes heavily disguised as the homosexual sheriff
bringing law and order to the West
oh but the ladies who ride that stagecoach want you to make love
    to
them but you never take off your shoes for fear you'll wake up
    only
to find a rattlesnake curled up in one of them.

Sometimes you
ride the stagecoach in another disguise.
You are in a black rubber diving suit
with your wet feet leaving prints like exotic fish on my forehead.
Under my hair is a brain
with
too many memory cells clicking off your name
trying to ascertain
your sex. I am swimming in Dry Gulch Hollow thinking of
    Sheriff
Stanley
who did love me but left to start the Pony Express.
His star I wear pinned to my black rubber skin-diving suit,
keeping clear of the 87 rattlesnakes swimming down the river
oh yes I catch this stagecoach you are on it Mr. Sheriff I would
    like
to be angry that we are not swimming in the same body of water
with every body of water suggesting so many more

the Pacific,
the Atlantic
the Indian,
Arctic, Antarctic
so many oceans about, not to mention the rivers, lakes, ponds,
    etc.

Shall we go skin-diving I ask you but it is
clear I want to explore different areas, my own black rubber suit
showing clearly
I am a woman
why did I find you? Black Aberdeen might walk in the
ocean, or Snowfoot stroll in coral reefs
but I am looking for the most beautiful fish,
one that will shimmer his scales at me and feed me special algae,
one with spiny teeth or soft train whistles,
shiny with tamarind seeds,
metaphysical with telephone books.
Found you writing your poems on my brain with the diving fork
    and
blood covering my suit with the words,
found you trapped in Dry Gulch Hollow settling for trout,
found you and wanted to have you, willing to lock you in my jail
    with a
big iron key, wanted to say look I have found him give me the
    reward
look I have found him and he'll take me away to his territory I
    am not
afraid of rattlesnakes they sleep with me at night curled
around my warm neck we exchange poisons oh Mr. Sheriff with
    sand on
your eyes with coyotes running out of your shoulders with
    scorpions
in your fingers with overhand knots and loop knots and granny
    knots
and reef knots and bowline knots and trefoil knots and a double
    bowknot

Incident of Cherries and Peaches

When the difference is not a name,
but is more than a name,
a whole concept,
as the Milky Way is
not looking out at a band of light
but looking out,
perspective-wise,
through a sphere,
a flattish disk,

then the difference is important.
To be scrupulous about the difference,
a must.
A consistency of view,
an inch to the mile, if you will,
but consistency,
most of all,
consistency is wanted.

Simultaneity: its importance;
where the differences must be scrupulous
in order to understand the overlap.

I have told you before,
the story;
the desert.
How flat and empty.
How dry.
How a bag of oranges has dried up
and the fruit are now as husks.
How the burlap bag bumps the legs of the donkey
as we cross the desert,
and the dried oranges rattle together inside like nuts.
How I walk along through the sand, leading the donkey.
How it dries your body to a husk.

How the bag and the oranges are husks.
How no one can go through the desert
and come out with any life.
How the dried up oranges will never revive.

At the same time, I must tell you of two men.
One man is standing on a plateau.
Another man is standing on another plateau
four hundred feet higher.
The man on Plateau A feels a great gust of wind
and is blown over.
But on Plateau B there is no wind.
Plateau B is above the wind.
The man stands and enjoys the quiet.

Sometimes I also tell it this way.
One man is standing on a plateau.
Another man is standing on a plateau
four hundred feet higher.
The man on Plateau A feels a great gust of wind
and is blown over.
There is no wind below on Plateau B.
It is beneath the wind
That man stands there and enjoys the silence.

But one way I have never told the story is this:
Eating fruit,
cherries and peaches,
I ride the donkey
in the desert.
His saddlebags are stuffed with fruit—
oranges, peaches, grapes, cherries, bananas.
When it is night we stop on a plateau called "Beautiful."
I lie down on the sand
which is still full of sun.
I look at the stars.
The Milky Way is to the south in the sky.

Ordinary Poem

"Where does the rain come from?
Oceans are the chief sources of rain
but lakes and other sources of water also contribute to it.
The heat of the sun evaporates water into the atmosphere.
There it remains as invisible vapor until it is con-
densed, first into clouds, and then into raindrops.
This happens
when the air is cooled (*see* Clouds; evaporation; water)."
                    Compton's Pictured Encyclopedia
                    Vol. 12, p. 88.

Where does the sun come from?
You are the chief source of sun,
but when you are not around, thinking of you contributes to it.
If I were metaphysical
I could say that everything revolves around you
and that makes a system
but I am not metaphysical.

Where do you come from?
You come from history, as everyone
comes from history.
This happens
when the air is cooled (*see* History; evolution; man) and
rain is made
which comes from the sun
which is all of us
because we live for the sun.

When it is raining
we feel drops
sometimes.
Sometimes
we feel larger masses.
Sometimes we feel rain when it is raining

and sometimes we feel
lots of water
which we know is rain
but feels more like water
than rain.

When the sun is shining
we feel warm.
Sometimes we feel warmer.
Then we feel hot.
When we get very hot,
we start feeling wet.
This is not the wet feeling of rain
or even of larger masses of water.
This is the wet feeling of heat.
Thus heat
hotness
of sun
could be said to produce a certain feeling of water.
Thus when the sun shines,
we feel warm,
then hot,
then water.

Where does this water come from?
Oceans are a chief source of rain.
But this water we have already
said
is not rain.
Rain is in drops,
cool.
Rain is ordinary
The sun is ordinary.
You are ordinary.
At least
as ordinary as the rain or the sun
But I don't think you are ordinary

like
this writing is
or poems
or the forms everything takes.
Even my love for you is ordinary—
at least as ordinary as
rain or the sun.
That is what I like best about
it.
I love you very much because you are not ordinary.

Where does love come from?
Oceans are the chief source of rain
but lakes and other sources of water also contribute to it.
The heat of the sun evaporates rain into the atmosphere.
There it remains as invisible vapor until it is con-
densed, first into clouds, and then into raindrops.
This happens
when the air is cooled.

All of this about rain and sun should relate
to love
because they are all so ordinary
and it is ordinary for poets
to make comparisons like this.
But if you do not find relationships,
that is ordinary too.
Since, the sun is the sun.
Rain is rain.
And they all mean whatever they mean.
                              The end.

1963

George Washington Writes Home About
Harvesting His Hemp

I won't take a lot of shit
in the name of love,
smoking it
or eating it,
or shoveling it
for you.

You write a letter to Martha,
telling her how much you miss her,
sitting at home, tight as a cable
managing your house.
How you long to be there
when the plants are harvested,
the special crops you spent long
hours reading the seed catalogue about—
    "makes especially fine
    thick
    resinous
    fibers"
said the book,
so juicy at harvest time
you smell the medicine
in the air.

And so you make special plans to be there
when the hemp is harvested:
your dreams take the form of women
lying down, taking off their clothes
on American flags,
serving you in the name of your country,
the soft aroma of Virgin-
ia hemp curling around your nose
like a cat rubbing at the cook's legs
while she's making dinner.

My first statement is true
about you and me:
the plants are ready to be harvested;
the hemp sticky with brown dust,
as a caterpillar
and you nostalgic,
away from your plantation,
coming in letters to remind
us of your deep commitments there.

But I'll let all that hemp die;
the ropes it will make
mean nothing to me — but nooses.
I will not take any more shit
in the name of love —
not smoke it,
or eat it,
or clean it up for you.

1965

Patriotic Poem

George Washington, your name is on my lips.
You had a lot of slaves.
I don't like the idea of slaves. I know I am
a slave to
too many masters, already
a red cardinal flies out of the pine tree in my eye swooping
down to crack a nut and the bird feeds on a tray draped with
a thirteen-starred flag. Underneath my heart where the fat clings
like bits of wool
I want to feel a man slipping his hand inside my body
massaging the heart, bathing
it in stripes, streams of new blood with stars floating in it
must pass through my arteries, each star pricking
the walls of veins with the prickly sensation of life.
The blood is old,
perhaps was shipped from Mt. Vernon
which was once a blood factory.
Mr. Washington, the pseudo aristocrat with two large fish
        instead of
feet, slapping around the plantation,
managing the country with surveyor's tools,
writing documents with sweet potatoes, yams, ham hocks, and
        black-eyed peas,
oh I hate southern gentlemen, too bad he was one;
somehow I've always hated the men who ran my country
but I was a loyal citizen. "Take me to your leader,"
and I'll give him a transfusion of my AB negative blood with stars
floating in it. I often said this
in a spirit of devotion, chauvinistic passion,
pining secretly for the beautiful Alexander Hamilton but making
        do with George who, after all, was the first president
and I need those firsts. On my wall, yes the wall of my
        stomach;
on my money, yes play money and real money, money I spend
        and money

42

I save, in and out of pocket; on documents, and deeds, statuary,
    monu-
ments, books, pictures, trains, old houses, whiskey bottles, and
    even
sewing machine shuttles there is his name
and my commitment, after all, is to names, how else, to what else
do we commit ourselves but names
and George I have committed myself to you. No Western sheriffs
    for me;
they only really like men and horses and sometimes gun play.
I guess I'm stuck with you, George, despite your absolute inability
to feel anything personal, or communicate it,
or at least share it with me.
Thank you at least for being first in your white linen and black
    coat.
My body, the old story, is my country, the only territory I
    control
and it certainly has been torn by wars. I'd like to think the
Revolution is over and that at last I am going to have my first
    pres-
ident, at last I can have an inaugural ball;
the white house of my corpuscles
asks for new blood; I have given so many transfusions to others
When will you make me your first lady, George?
When will I finally become the first president's wife?

1964

The Father of My Country

All fathers in Western civilization must have
a military origin. The
ruler,
governor,
yes,
he is
was the
general at one time or other.
And George Washington
won the hearts
of his country—the rough military man
with awkward
sincere
drawing-room manners.

My father;
have you ever heard me speak of him? I seldom
do. But I had a father,
and he had military origins—or my origins from
him
are military,
militant. That is, I remember him only in uniform. But of the
    navy,
30 years a chief petty officer,
always away from home.

It is rough/hard for me to speak
now.
I'm not used to talking
about him.
Not used to naming his objects/
objects
that never surrounded me.

A woodpecker with fresh bloody crest
knocks

at my mouth. Father, for the first
time I say
your name. Name rolled in thick Polish parchment scrolls,
name of Roman candle drippings when I sit at my table
alone, each night,
name of naval uniforms and name of
telegrams, name of
coming home from your aircraft carrier,
name of shiny shoes.
name of Hawaiian dolls, name
of mess spoons, name of greasy machinery, and name of
stencilled names.
Is it your blood I carry in a test tube,
my arm,
to let fall, crack, and spill on the sidewalk
in front of the men
I know,
I love,
I know, and
want? So you left my house when I was under two.
being replaced by other machinery (my sister), and
I didn't believe you left me.

           This scene: the trunk yielding treasures of
           a green fountain pen, heart shaped mirror,
           amber beads, old letters with brown ink, and
           the gopher snake stretched across the palm tree
           in the front yard with woody trunk like monkey skins,
           and a sunset through the skinny persimmon trees. You
           came walking, not even a telegram or post card from
           Tahiti. Love, love, through my heart like ink in
           the thickest nibbed pen, black and flowing into words
           You came, to me, and I at least six. Six doilies
           of lace, six battleship cannon, six old beerbottles,
           six thick steaks, six love letters, six clocks
           running backwards, six watermelons, and six baby
           teeth, a six cornered hat on six men's heads, six
           lovers at once or one lover at sixes and sevens;

how I confuse
all this with my
dream
walking the tightrope bridge
with gold knots
over
the mouth of an anemone/tissue spiral lips
and holding on so that the ropes burned
as if my wrists had been tied

If George Washington
had not
been the Father
of my Country
it is doubtful that I would ever have
found
a father. Father in my mouth, on my lips, in my
tongue, out of all my womanly fire,
Father I have left in my steel filing cabinet as a name on my birth
certificate, Father I have left in the teeth pulled out at
dentists' offices and thrown into their garbage cans,
Father living in my wide cheekbones and short feet,
Father in my Polish tantrums and my American speech, Father,
    not a
holy name, not a name I cherish but the name I bear, the name
that makes me one of a kind in any phone book because
you changed it, and nobody
but us
has it,
Father who makes me dream in the dead of night of the falling
    cherry
blossoms, Father who makes me know all men will leave me
if I love them,
Father who made me a maverick,
a writer,
a namer,
name/father, sun/father, moon/father, bloody mars/father,

46

other children said, "My father is a doctor,"
or
"My father gave me this camera,"
or
"My father took me to
the movies,"
or
"My father and I went swimming,"
but
my father is coming in a letter
once a month
for a while,
and my father
sometimes came in a telegram
but
mostly
my father came to me
in sleep, my father because I dreamed in one night that I dug
through the ash heap in back of the pepper tree and found a
        diamond
shaped like a dog, and my father called the dog and it came
        leaping
over to him and he walked away out of the yard down the road
        with
the dog jumping and yipping at his heels,

my father was not in the telephone book
in my city;
my father was not sleeping with my mother
at home;
my father did not care if I studied the
piano;
my father did not care what
I did;
and I thought my father was handsome and I loved him and I
        wondered
why

he left me alone so much,
so many years
in fact, but
my father made me what I am,
a lonely woman,
without a purpose, just as I was
a lonely child
without any father. I walked with words, words, and names,
names. Father was not
one of my words.
Father was not
one of my names. But now I say, "George, you have become my
      father,
in his 20th century naval uniform. George Washington, I need
      your
love; George, I want to call you Father, Father, my Father,"
Father of my country,
that is,
me. And I say the name to chant it. To sing it. To lace it around
me like weaving cloth. Like a happy child on that shining
      afternoon
in the palmtree sunset with her mother's trunk yielding treasures,
I cry and
cry,
Father,
Father,
Father,
have you really come home?

1964

George Washington Slept Here

Scattered
in the barnyard
fading into the stained color of old bureau drawers
bones from many
dismembered chickens
lay
almost concealed by the barnyard dust.
The place, transformed
by its new owners,
had lost the tumbledown look of a chicken farm. It was in fact
the home of the retired
president
of our country. No. 1 Uno. The first.
ola, or u, whatever word ending would indicate
specialness.
He came for a southern fried chicken dinner
and mint juleps. He fell asleep in the swing and he stayed. They
put his name on the door and said Washington
slept here.
   Here in this place
   you and I slept. We dreamed
   in unison
   of the grey battleships
   They came secretly into the harbor
   and in fatigues you watched them lining up
   cannons, missiles, the accoutrements
   of war.
   But a pair of red shoes
   stained red from a gaping hole in my arm
   was sitting on deck
   tiny, pointed, high-heeled,
   and the gunners could not miss them,
   threw them
   overboard.
   With one arm around me

in love,
devotion,
the other was smashing the back of my head with
a rock.
Man in the grey uniform,
man that I still love,
man who makes me weep in the stomach as I walk
calmly thru the world,
we slept together long enough to be joined at
the thigh bone,
and the dream offers no hope
with the ocean turning to blood from those
stained abandoned shoes.
The open declarations of love
must turn on themselves,
must attack me,
must tattoo my mouth with pain.
I am afraid of talk,
having once said
"I love you," and not wanting to repeat
such a mistake.

George Washington slept here
in this very bed. They put on clean white sheets
for him
and a warming pan into the
iron-cold bed.
An interest in history divulged the maker
of the bed—
one A. Johnson Peabody by name, old carver of wood,
designer of simple sturdy frames.
History will also tell you the date,
1794,
a year when the music box came over from France
and one new harmonium.
The chairs made in this new colony
were more beautiful than high court furniture of Louis Quinze.

Oh Washington,
you slept here,
you left the imprint of your tired head
in the goosey pillow.
My own historical bed is empty without you,
father of my country.
Your eagle
appears in the night to pull out all my hidden currency
from drawers and closets
and then flaps over my narrow bed once.
I dream of you just vaguely
sailing on the Mediterranean with a black-headed woman
whose hair is filled with snakes,
dancing in Sweden with a black-haired woman whose belly is
filled with ice,
bicycling in Germany with the black-headed woman whose eyes
    are
melted lead.
You travel with her away from your country, your history,
and I sit by the fire in winter
chatting with
Betsy Ross
as she sews me a new dress
made from the American flag.
George Washington slept here is written
over the fireplace
but the fire burns now
without any of the wood from his historic
cherry tree.

1964

Uncle Sam in the White House

Silver grapes in sleeves
            showering their teeth under feet
                    silver tape
    binding the sun, keeping
                    it inside my knees
                        making my steps shaky
Silver stars taped
    to my lips
            the silver stripes bind me
                    each part of my body rests
            wrapped in flags
    in a silvery, sparkling drawer
                sometimes I see my eyes
in the sidewalk.

When Uncle Sam moved into the White House
            the whole country applauded
                    its old hero
    and was glad that silver-haired Uncle Sam
                was the first Negro American president.

He redecorated the house in silver
    and my silver knee and elbow bones
            with all their jangling keys
were slipped into his pockets

See how patriotic I am,
    the genuine daughter of
            George Washington,
a silvery key, sometimes a dime or a
    quarter, always a hard little
            click
in the pocket or desk drawer
    of Uncle Sam,
our newly elected Negro president —

         tiptoe past the silver carpets
outside his door. A little silver ghost
     like a spoon
and he won't let me
    in.

1964

George Washington: The Whole Man

The disappointment I am talking of now
comes without heartbreak or the
malfunctioning of body and brain,
comes through the hope of communication
and follows the lack of it.
I had hoped you would live up to my idea
of the great man
but found myself disappointed on every level.

I. RETICENCE   *for J.*

Sitting at your drawing board
sketching plans for Mt. Vernon
you, as I can remember, fade into that Swede I idealized
Mt. Vernon is typical of the wealthy planter aristocracy style
(or so it says in the book)
and you walk through woods
as tranquilly as/or corridors.
The summer of 1785 brought the
leaf eaters
and tree blight
and no rain. You lost your black gum,
pine,
locust,
poplar,
mulberry,
crab apple,
papaw,
cedar,
hemlock,
and sassafras.
Your imported golden pheasants languished
and when you laid out a deer park,
the deer continually escaped & gnawed away
your saplings.

As much as you worked, your aristocratic lands were
tight-lipped
(much as you are)
communicating not to your fingers. You learned silence
from the torrid summers and the unreachable land
beyond the Alleghenies.
Holding an icy glass
you mediate between desire and responsibility. Like the good
man, you
never choose the easy life.

George, I remember a walk we took through
someone else's lush park
and you asked
how he did it. His fortunes were
in his land, I said,
and you closed your mouth silently
as if it were hinged,
knowing neither your body nor
your land would yield much pleasure,
neither respond to the touch of
a spade or a rake.

We walked over brooks, through
Japonica gardens, and finally to the arched
white gazebo.
Your buckled shoes were dusty and I remember
the tired look as you touched my hand,
lace emerging from your cuff.
We talked of each plant in detail
and yet you never told me
once
anything
about yourself.
The reticence of a man
who had
never learned to talk.

II. THE CLASSICAL CODE   *for R.*

"When Lafayette sent him the key of the Bastille, to symbolize
the overthrow of despotism, Washington responded merely with
a polite acknowledgement and a token gift in return.
                    Not for the value of the thing, my dear
                    Marquis, but as a memorial, and because
                    they are the manufacture of this city, I
                    send you herewith a pair of shoe-buckles.
A pair of shoe-buckles—what inspired flatness."

                    Marcus Cunliffe, *George Washington,*
                    Man and Monument, p. 160

and this makes you seem classical, most of all.

I should trim my hair straight across
I should find pleasure in only the straight line.
I should cut out all curves
and melodies
all close connections
and off-beat poses.
I should think of the effect
and should find pleasure only in a
pure
process.
I should designate the goals simply
and be sparing about my sex life.
I should know a great deal
keep it all to myself
and believe in only that which will last.
Shit.
Life upsets those patterns when we are 18/or at least
my life has.
I want to embrace the ephemeral
as tightly, as spontaneously,
as often

as the historical, classical, and great.
My life is definitely not one long bicycle ride
or one long
anything else.
It is a cold hard fact.
It is true we are too easily impressed
by someone's impeccably good taste.

George, you did all the right things,
but you hardly seemed alive.
They all said you were dull or hard to talk to,
and of course THAT
isn't classical; so thank god I can
tell you this.
I am pissed off at you for being so easily convinced
by what seem like weak arguments.
Still, it is with pleasure I
remember the shoe buckles
and with pleasure I see
how you've used Lafayette's key.

III. PATHOS   *for G*

Whether it is historical or not I cannot say. The protagonist
so to speak was someone famous—
George Washington, to be truthful, who first fell in love with
Betsy Fauntleroy when he was 20
and she, a belle, did not like his manners.
He gave her, I believe,
for I dreamed this and there is no better verifier than the dream,
a glass aquarium containing
18 lizards,
each a different species,
one green sunning itself on a waxy magnolia leaf,
another translucent amber showing the cartilage of the body
as the stick in a clear sucker shows through,
still another black like a tire and rough and contrasting with the

prettiness of the glass and the others.
18 lizards in their glass box.
Hardly calculated to win the embroidered heart of Betsy
     Fauntleroy,
her powdered wig slipped awry with astonishment
at such a gift.

George, in and out of time, your historical hands
that should sign great documents move over my body,
into my brain,
squeezing the thalamus,
fingering the spongy protrusions that make me dream,
cerebellum, lifting each part away from the other to explore
all the channels, George of many
perceptions, your life
touched me in a way I respond to no one else.
The image, identity of myself;
George, you have come to recite the constitution in me in my
sleep.
The words soothe my brain that you earlier explored.

IV. TRIUMPH   *for D.*

The last time I called the White House and left a message for you
was shortly after you had decided to retire.
You were sitting in your study with the wig off.
You, in fact, had just come from Mexico and an image that the
     public
never discovered was apparent:
The snake curling around your neck into your velvet coat,
and the gold Aztec sun trying to draw out your heart with metal
     teeth.
George, you dreamed the sun sucked out your heart
infusing itself with red as it set.
Occasionally, in those last days a cock fight would be set up
in a mahogany room. To bet on the strutter
you had special coins minted,

58

one side picturing the cock's beak as a weapon in Hercules' hand,
the other side giving the eye of the rooster, an eye that
could see into the pocket where it rested,
an eye that would give no rest to anyone that held it.
Transforming your cold life,
the bony moon coming out of the kitchen while sun fills your
    genitals
and begs someone other than Martha to give you one last
    embrace.
How often we ought to rewrite history,
connections often being made at the wrong time,
facts not consistent with the factors.
George, I would rewrite your history in a hot country
with desert, snakes, and a sip of Rio Grande water.
In triumph we see the great man covered with gold.

1964

Blue Monday

Blue of the heaps of beads poured into her breasts
and clacking together in her elbows;
blue of the silk
that covers lily-town at night;
blue of her teeth
that bite cold toast
and shatter on the streets;
blue of the dyed flower petals with gold stamens
hanging like tongues
over the fence of her dress
at the opera/opals clasped under her lips
and the moon breaking over her head a
gush of blood-red lizards.

Blue Monday. Monday at 3:00 and
Monday at 5. Monday at 7:30 and
Monday at 10:00. Monday passed under the rippling
California fountain. Monday alone
a shark in the cold blue waters.

       You are dead: wound round like a paisley shawl.
       I cannot shake you out of the sheets. Your name
       is still wedged in every corner of the sofa.

       Monday is the first of the week,
       and I think of you all week.
       I beg Monday not to come
       so that I will not think of you
       all week.

You paint my body blue. On the balcony
in the softy muddy night, you paint me
with bat wings and the crystal
the crystal
the crystal

the crystal in your arm cuts away
the night, folds back ebony whale skin
and my face, the blue of new rifles,
and my neck, the blue of Egypt,
and my breasts, the blue of sand,
and my arms, bass-blue,
and my stomach, arsenic;

there is electricity dripping from me like cream;
there is love dripping from me I cannot use—like acacia or
jacaranda—fallen blue and gold flowers, crushed into the street.

> Love passed me in a blue business suit
> and fedora.
> His glass cane, hollow and filled with
> sharks and whales . . .
> He wore black
> patent leather shoes
> and had a mustache. His hair was so black
> it was almost blue.
>
> "Love," I said.
> "I beg your pardon," he said.
> "Mr. Love," I said.
> "I beg your pardon," he said.
>
> So I saw there was no use bothering him on the
>   street
>
> Love passed me on the street in a blue
> business suit. He was a banker
> I could tell.

So blue trains rush by in my sleep.
Blue herons fly overhead.
Blue paint cracks in my
arteries and sends titanium

floating into my bones.
Blue liquid pours down
my poisoned throat and blue veins
rip open my breast. Blue daggers tip
and are juggled on my palms.
Blue death lives in my fingernails.

If I could sing one last song
with water bubbling through my lips
I would sing with my throat torn open,
the blue jugular spouting that black shadow pulse,
and on my lips
I would balance volcanic rock
emptied out of my veins. At last
my children strained out
of my body. At last my blood
solidified and tumbling into the ocean.
It is blue.
It is blue.
It is blue.

1964

Rescue Poem

When he diagnosed
my case,
it left me with little
hope.
"You have an invisible telephone booth
around you,"
he said.
"It is the glass hard cardamon whispers cannot penetrate.
Glass of cut-out tongues
and spider tracks,
of the turn of a bolt one thread
and of the distance one hammer-blow drives a nail.
The space of a snake's forehead
and the diamond ladder of a window washer.
A shadow foot between the real foot and the ground."

He smiles at my disease,
says he would like to put his arms around me
but cannot
reach around the whole invisible telephone
booth.
We walk through the night
trailing lizards.
Our heads are filled
with fat wet moss.
Black camels walk around
and through our eyes
stamping on the city streets.
We thread needles with our thin bones
and sew streets together
trying to hold them in finger pockets.

"I cannot get near you," he said. "That telephone booth
being in the way." In the way really
was the dial

tone—
the sound of ruby acorns pelting a roof of elbows.
"Busy, busy,"
the help signal gone crazy
reaching to years of hurricane weather.

Here are the tools to chop down an invisible telephone booth:
      an apple inside the ear
      a bucket of blood
      a hammer made out of beetle tongues
      a saw made from parts of the cheek
      teeth chipped out of the navel
      diamond breasts and a silver penis
Well, you came with strange luggage,
a man from your own trust company,
a bag full of incredible instruments. You looked at
the doctor and said,
"I'm a specialist. Is she
the one with the invisible telephone booth?
She the one nobody can get near?
She the one who stands naked inside it, making
long distance calls for help?
and has line-men out everyday wrecking
their instruments on this invisible glass?"

Yes, you had a bag with
    apples rolling inside your ears,
        shaking their seeds into Eustachian tubes
        and down alimentary canals,
      buckets of blood were capped with silver
        fish skins and sloshed inside the black bag,
      carrying hundreds of small initials,
      your hammer of cricket tongues
        tapped itself to sleep
        waiting for the big job,
      the saw made of all the soft parts of
        a cheek sharpened itself against eyebrows,

teeth chipped out of the navel were
        ready to bite
and diamond breasts with hard nipples
        rubbed against the silver penis
        causing the fish eyes to glow
You set to work at once
on the telephone booth.
        Need I say the obvious?
        That you found the door?
        That no one else had tried the obvious?
        Need I say more?
        An obvious solution to an obvious problem.
        Come in.
        Put in your silver nickel,
        your pennies,
        quarters,
        dimes.
        Come inside
        these invisible walls.

        Join me
        on the silver
        wirey
        inside.

1964

Sun

Under my elbow. In my elbow.
Under my bed. In my bed.
Under my foot. In my foot.
Under my eye. In my eye.

        Yes. Yes. I've found it.
The lost key, key, key, key, key, key—
What bird sings that song
        Key, key

A bird made out of keys,
flying to unlock the sun. let out the heat.
flying to unlock the moon. and let out the milk.
flying to unravel the mountain.
and resting on a branch saying,
key, key.

1963

3 of Swords
—for dark men under the white moon

Yes,
of old wire hangers that remain in the closet,
of the Satsuma plum tree you crawled out of the window to
     (in the dark
     after they thought their ten-year-old child was asleep
     but was
     resting in the branches
     like a cat who knows where to sit himself
     silkily
     down
     resting surrounded by leaves
     rustling like many hands dealing cards swiftly)
Yes,
of the moon in her wet menstrual period
lacing rust streaks across a crater,
of the dust in the old lady's hairnet,
of running the greyhound in the closet where he can only move
½ of a leap,
of grubby fingers shooting the white aggie,
of a pot of soup on a cold night—
     pictures of . . .
     in the moon's bloodshot eye;
     your sleep is ghost sleep.
     No wonder you are always tired;
     you run
     the coyote with his ragged smelly hunger
     in my dreams every night.
     I watch you
     pacing
     in the rim of the hills
     I watch you
     stealing
     delicately
     even from the bullet-marked foot.

Asters grow in the backyard,
some under your bed.
What we never speak of is that
I love too many men
and would not be unfaithful to myself.
I am the sword with
the starry hilt.
Dream of me. I love you in a rain of grey paint
as I love the coyote for his stealing
and the lonely Westerner for his silver bullets,
and all George Washingtons—1st and last—
and the men who hold out that wild card
—the three of swords—
not knowing
my heart melts and bleeds and runs
for their steel;
it sings for piercing
and it accepts hungrily the knife;
it comes for its exercise in a bed made
of swords
and asks, genuinely, to be rebathed
in thick plasma each night.

How can I tell you
the moon was made to shine alone each night
walking to her bath and undressing alone.
Her breasts spout milk
and her children slide down from the sky.
Her lovers she nibbles and whispers to,
sends messages by the wind to touch their ears,
takes, allows herself to be taken calmly
each day
away.

Oh how can I tell you, she loves you,
but wants to be alone,
wants to be in your wrist,

a pulse,
but not in your house. See,
she is outside the window now.
You look at her.
It does not mean you should try
to bring her inside.

1964

Ringless

I cannot stand the man who wears
a ring
on his little finger/a white peacock walking on the moon
and splinters of silver dust his body;
but the great man, George, cracked in half in my living room
one day and I saw he was made of marble
with black veins. It does not justify the ring to say
someone gave it to you and the little finger is the only one
it will fit;
it does not justify to say Cocteau wore one
and still made the man burst silently through the mirror—
many beautiful
poems have been made with rings worn on the little finger.
That
isn't the point.
Flaubert had jasper; Lorca had jade; Dante had
amber; and Browning had carnelian;
George Washington had solid gold—even Kelly once wore a
    scarab there;
but I am telling you I cannot stand the man
who wears a ring
on his little finger. He may indeed
run the world;
that does not make him any better in
my needlepoint eyes.
Why
is a story.

> There were heaps of fish lying, shimmering in the sun
> with red gashes still heaving
> and the mouths of medieval lovers.
> There were gold and green glass balls bobbing in their
> nets on the waves.
> There were black-eyed men with hair all over their bodies
> There were black-skirted ladies baking bread
> and there were gallons and gallons of red wine.

A girl spilled one drop of hot wax on her lover's neck
as she glanced at his white teeth and thick arms.
There were red and silver snakes coiling around the legs
of the dancers.
There was hot sun and there was no talk.
How do I reconcile these images with our cool president,
George Washington, walking the streets? Every bone
in my body is ivory and has the word "America"
carved on it, but
my head takes me away from furniture and pewter
to the sun tugging at my nipples and trying to squeeze
under my toes.
The sun appeared in the shape of a man and he had
a ring made of sun around his little finger.
"It will burn up your hand," I said.
But he made motions in the air and passed by.
The moon appeared in the shape of a young Negro boy,
and he had a ring made of dew around his little finger.
"You'll lose it," I said,
but he touched my face,
not losing a drop and passed away. Then I saw
Alexander Hamilton, whom I loved,
and he had a ring on his little finger,
but he wouldn't touch me.
And Lorca had rings around both little fingers,
and suddenly everyone I knew appeared,
and they all had rings on their little fingers,
and I was the only one in the world left without any
rings
on any
of my fingers whatsoever.
And worst of all,
there was George Washington
walking down the senate aisles
with a ring on his little finger—managing
the world,
managing *my* world.

This is what I mean—you wear a ring on your
little finger
and you manage the world,
and I am ringless
ringless . . .
I cannot stand the man who wears
a ring on his little finger;

not even if it is you.

c. 1966

Slicing Oranges for Jeremiah

as the juice ran out on the wooden board
      the third orange you had cut for this son of yours
      opened
      and he grabbed the slices like a little raccoon running to
      prepare them,
      carrying his bowl to the table where he ate,
his instinct trying to make up for something not in his throat
or his fingers,
trying to make up for the thyroid gland he was born without
      he would eat a dozen oranges if you would let him
rosy Jeremiah, with long eyelashes

what does it mean
if a child cannot talk when he is six,
if he shits in the toilet one day, in his pants the next?
what does it mean
if a man drinks and can't earn enough money?
and what if he tells his wife he'd like another woman
but wouldn't have one,
and what does it mean
if he tells his wife she's unpleasant or dull
and what
does
it mean
if his wife takes sleeping pills or walks
in front of a car?
and what
does it mean,
if Jeremiah takes the sun
and slices it up
like the oranges and eats a little fire
thirsty for the juice?

When you take the knife in your hand
to slice an orange first into quarters, then into eighths,

73

each slice shining—
        as orange jelly, a goldfish,
        lights on the water at night,
and you cut, competently, efficiently, a housewife
who knows how to divide,
when you take your instrument and use it
making pools of orange juice, letting the peel spray into
your nostrils,
what does it mean?
                And your son,
eating orange after orange,
until I felt the juice in my own mouth,
just watching,
and the sweetness,
and I wondered what was missing,
or why,
and where his thyroid went
or why there was no gland there,
and how even this baby animal,
your son,
must know that it was you who kept him alive,
remembering his pill each day,
and taking him places where people would respect him
and letting him make drawings
and build garbage structures:
and how his father knew too
it was you who kept him, your husband, alive,
giving him whatever artificial gland it was you did each day,
and how they both resented it,
depending on it as they did,
the men needing the woman more than any man could admit.

And what does it mean,
this strength you have?
It keeps you hovering towards death.
It keeps you near the pill bottles and close to the wheels of cars.
It keeps you sad and compassionate,

willing to understand the miseries of others.
It isn't weakness that points us towards death,
but strength, men dying earlier than women,
trying to show their strength,
women taking their own lives with gas, in ovens with their
gold-clock babies under their aprons,
with sleeping pills glistening like amber necklaces poured into
the stomach's cave,
stepping quietly under car wheels,
as they lie with their men at night,
not murmuring,
enduring
until the breath is pushed out.

Slicing oranges for your son,
you cannot see what I see,
the oranges growing outside my own back door when I was five,
the dusty dark citrus leaves making black smudges
against my sweater.
There is a gypsy in me
who wants to run
with all these oranges in a bag
and trade them for the sun
or find someone who will cut them for me
the way you slice them for Jeremiah.
That care;
that efficiency.
Instead of some gland, I might have
an orange tree
growing just behind my throat
straining to stay alive, to endure,
waiting for the efficient hand to reach inside
and slice the oranges
as you do,
as I saw you
slice oranges for Jeremiah,

slice the oranges for your son
who could eat a dozen you said
if you'd let him.

1966

Filling the Boxes of Joseph Cornell

Aren't we nasty little people
looking at treasure boxes?
         here is one having a pair of chocolate legs
         in high heels,
         a silver mirror,
         a beef tongue, slightly purplish
         and streaked, like meat turning bad,
and only wanting to
change their contents;
fill them with ourselves?

      The structure of anger
      is repetition;
      tell him over and over you saw the girl he raped
      and killed, her face streaked purple
      large blotches on her breasts,
      part of the hand severed
      and thrown across the room,
      and over and over you tell him
      yelling at him about how you saw her and what he
      did, and how you hate him and how he took someone's
      life, and the structure of your anger
      is *only* repetition,
      of all the ugly things,
      over and over . . .

        (I'll say, "he hurt me,
        he hurt me,"
        over and over,
        thinking about the assault,
        trying to make it go away
        out of my head
        all memory of him leave me.

we are standing outside of a window displaying
electronic equipment. $100 for this small speaker,
$300 for this turntable. $400 for this amplifier.
You can scarcely contain yourself, wanting all these beautiful
square boxlike parts that will make sounds slip into your
ears like a beautiful pair of hands.

When I used to go to the movies on Friday nights with my
mother and sister in Whittier, California, we used to see the
previews of coming attractions, and even though I knew
that we went to the movies every week-end, I
could scarcely sit in my seat,
wanting so physically to be there, seeing the new movie
in color perhaps with Betty Grable wearing chocolate colored
stockings and sitting in her dressing room looking at
the mirror, while the rich ugly man
brought her flowers and the poor handsome
man waited outside.

Whose tongue was hanging out for her?

Your tongue hanging out for new hi-fi equipment.
No matter where we see the scenes, we are structuring
the parts we like, putting them into little stagelike boxes
of our own, with our own additions —
          some ostrich feathers,
          a silver inkwell,
          a dime bank, a photo of a countess,
          a graduation certificate;
fill them ourselves, as if the world had no artistry,
no sense of placement, no choice
settling things where they were settled.
                    The old man, my kind father-in-law,
                    saying after having painted watercolors for 20 years,
                    little landscapes and vases of flowers,
                    getting up at 5 in the morning to go into the city
                    and sketch for an hour before work

and whose only problem was that he had little
    talent—
though skill was something he knew about
and tried to perfect—
he said, as we drove through the country,
that he always changes the landscape when he paints
    it,
because there is no good arrangement in nature,
only he always changed it
by putting in the same barn,
the same two rocks,
and the same boat, even when there was no water,
the boat then being disguised as a bush

Aren't we nasty little people,
looking at boxes, never accepting what is there,
always putting in our own arrangements?

    The structure of anger
    is repetition. We are angered by people trying to
    arrange our lives for us—no structure we
    build being suitable for all others,
    the argument about whether this war is worse than
    all other wars—two pacifists militantly fighting about
    when it's right to kill, another pacifist
    saying how killing can only be evil,
    but letting his parents destroy him, kill him
    with softness and tenderness and kindness
    at an early age, and now he doing it to his own child,
    and she in anger, even as a 10-year-old, lashing
    out in anger, not learning to read, not learning to
    talk, not learning to keep herself clean, and secretly
    knowing what she is doing,
    killing,
    this repetition, over and over

The same poem, the same life, the same destructive relationships,
relating the color—if it's blue

I   am blue
I am blue as a blues singer
I am blue in the face from saying the same things over
        & over
I am blue because of you and what you've done to me
I am blue because it was my favorite color as a baby
(it didn't take much to teach me
that my parents wanted a boy
and the best adjustment I could make was to
like blue)

Little boy blue, come blow your horn
Sheep's in the meadow, cow's in the corn.

Repetition is the structure of anger.

You keep saying something over and over
and it goes away
or you go away from it,
ultimately being bored with too much of a good thing.

There is a man who keeps making boxes
and putting new and strange and beautiful things in them.
        a map of all the currents of all the oceans in the world
        and a silver instrument of steering a ship
        sometimes ladies' objects; sometimes men's.
        Never the same; never a repetition of subject,
        but always the box, over and over.

Repetition is what structures our lives . . . Where we find a unity
we find a work of art, some sense,
something we call a life?

For years I have been repeating formulae I learned to
keep my devils away; and now I don't have any devils, but I say
the same formulae when angels are around
and

of course
they go away too.

The structure of repetition is one that makes songs
and dances and boxes
        I don't want to repeat myself.
        It seems to be the only way of getting a point across
        though

Across the ocean I know someone who's repeating himself
and who repeated himself
        just as when someone doesn't hear you, they will
        ask you to repeat what you said,
        or there might be a repeat broadcast of something we liked
        on the radio, or you might have to repeat a course you
        failed in school or when you belch you are
        repeating your food.
        Mainly,
        repetition is for learning or for fear

Have I repeated myself enough? Little boy blue,
that's you.
I never turned out to be Little Boy Blue,
just a woman who likes blue a lot,
even the blues.
If I repeat your name three hundred times in a row
it will begin to sound absurd;
if I replayed our life together, all the scenes three hundred
times they too would seem absurd—but everything in the world
would, under such conditions

What I want most of all is to repeat your name
until you become something real,
not a fantasy.
What I want is a structure of repetition
that makes me angry,
makes me strong

(because, as Martha said, anger is a stronger emotion
in our culture).
For once,
I'd like to look at the artist's velvet-lined box
and enjoy his world.
My tongue is not large and purple and streaked with rot,
as his beef tongue.
Mine has smaller,
different things to say.

It is a mark of determination
or stupidity
to repeat your mistakes.

1966

The Hermit

With gravel glued together for arms and legs,
charcoal-blackened wood for feet,
hands,
the body a leather bolster,
head a hard ball—
        the withered dried up man who had
        eaten nothing but sweetened dew for 30 years
        knelt by the roadside.
        A robber attacked him from behind
        cutting down the old man with his knife.
        He put on the old man's ragged robe
        and himself began to pray.
        "Lord, Lord, I have killed a good man
        gratuitously. What shall I do?"
        But nothing happened.
        The old man's body began to rot.
        The robber sang and chanted.
        He forgot
        after some time
        his origins.

1965

An Apology

Past exchanges have left orbits of rain around my face,
Words used-up as the empty shell of the beetle.
    I did not mean to insult you,
        but perhaps wanted to scorch you with that steamy teakettle
        of my 2700 years,
        to tell you youth shouldn't be humble as the tablecloth,
        but arrogant and fierce/
    we get toothless with age;
    should bite hard when we're young.
To tell you not to follow masters whose egos are sponges,
To tell you not that you had nothing to say
    but that you need to pour it out at your own speed,
    in an empty space where it will knock against you.
I saw the dream of the tongue floating in a bowl of water
as a desperate sacrifice. You,
    giving up your own words,
You. giving up identity to float safely on display in
another man's ocean;
I saw everything that made me weep spools of rotten thread
for my own disconnected life —
    drop cement trowels from my knees and
    broken clocks from my elbows.
Wanting to discard the past; renege my own life, the pain
of recognition and hate mingles with the identity.
I apologize for lack of grace —
    not passing you with a zen stance.
Elders should be lacquered in their place.
And women commit their words
    to the dream code; toads & shooting stars in the blood,
    icy milk pails,
    snow,
    oranges,
    diamonds, eyes to the ground. Women should be
    silently riding their zebras.

1964

Sestina from the Home Gardener

These dried-out paint brushes which fell from my lips have been
    removed
with your departure; they are such minute losses
compared with the light bulb gone from my brain, the sections
of chicken wire from my liver, the precise
silver hammers in my ankles which delicately banged and pointed
magnetically to you. Love has became unfamiliar

and plenty of time to tend the paint brushes now. Once
    unfamiliar
with my processes. Once removed
from that sizzling sun, the ego, to burn my poet shadow to the
    wall, I pointed,
I suppose, only to your own losses
which made you hate that 200 pound fish called marriage. Precise
ly, I hate my life, hate its freedom, hate the sections

of fence stripped away, hate the time for endless painting, hate the
    sections
of my darkened brain that wait for children to snap on the light,
    the unfamiliar
corridors of my heart with strangers running in them, shouting.
    The precise
incisions in my hip to extract an image, a dripping pickaxe or
    palmtree removed
and each day my paint brushes get softer and cleaner—better tools,
    and losses
cease to mean loss. Beauty, to each eye, differently pointed.

I admire sign painters and carpenters. I like that black hand
    pointed
up a drive-way whispering to me. "The Washingtons live in those
    sections"
and I explain autobiographically that George Washington is
    sympathetic to my losses;

His face or name is everywhere. No one is unfamiliar
with the American dollar, and since you've been removed
from my life I can think of nothing else. A precise

replacement for love can't be found. But art and money are precise
ly for distraction. The stars popping out of my blood are pointed
nowhere. I have removed
my ankles so that I cannot travel. There are sections
of my brain growing teeth and unfamiliar
hands tie strings through my eyes. But there are losses

of the spirit like vanished bicycle tires and losses
of the body, like the whole bike, every precise
bearing, spoke, gear, even the unfamiliar
handbrakes vanished. I have pointed
myself in every direction, tried sections
of every map. It's no use. The real body has been removed.

Removed by the ice tongs. If a puddle remains what losses
can those sections of glacier be? Perhaps a precise
count of drops will substitute the pointed mountain, far away,
    unfamiliar?

c. 1964

The Ice Eagle

It was with resolution that she gave up the
powerful teardrops in her eyes—
that crystal, the Venus-soft lizard-eyed creature called woman,
    gazes
through, her philosopher's stone,
the sweet glass
that drops from the sky.
Ancients,
in sacrifice,
cut off tears
with knives.
*   *   *

The 50 lb. eagle carved out of ice
sitting in the silver punch bowl
turned her attention to physical details.
       Why am I saying
       "her"?
       It is I,
       undoubtedly I,
       the life a dream work.
Undoubtedly the life has been confused with the movies,
I, Gloria Swanson, walking discontented
for all parties become that to me. I cannot
walk through the rituals
without my golden mask,
alas, 3 dozen of them hang on my wall,
the thick lips reminding me of what has been eaten
and has not nourished.

Physical details: the lawn that sloped down to the sea cliffs,
the swallows building their nests in rafters,
the stone house punctured with courts and patios,
Bougainvillea winding up its sides,
raw old Spanish wood composing chests and high still chairs

moved and touched into water-like smoothness,
the gravel driveway balancing the cutaway heels
of beautiful women,
the men swimming through the night in dinner jackets like
    paper cups
floating on the ocean;
yes, her eyes—
        again why do I say
        "her,"
        I must insist it is I—
my eyes are informed of silk and the obsidian minds of the rich.
Here is a thick glossy black smooth idea—sex and nothing else.
The rich are born bored
and look for purposes, causes, projects
to keep them busy.
The women make up wild malachite eyes, green with beautiful
sleep and restless knowledge of new plays,
new dancers,
new books,
new jazz. They
can ring their Egyptian eyes with kohl
and be aesthetes
and in veils walk down the rocky path to the sea,
riding black tigers of Sartre and Camus and Ionesco,
yards of chiffon trailing their heels and they despair
the men,
they, I, we
        all women when it gets past social class
despair the men who have only the moon in their milky fluid
    fingers.
Yes, they wait,
the sun god we wait,
to find him naked in a blaze of fire.
We are stuck with vulgar substitutes—
the fashionable avant-garde dancer,
the sensational beat poet,
the jazz trumpeter,

the Negro novelist,
and Amen-ra, Amen-ra, our father, they are all glorious
    sun-brilliant
artists, but
homosexuals
fucking each other, riding on their own black panthers
wading into the iron waters.
Again the women must rest their bodies against each other and
    moan.
It is not the mysteries that draw the men,
but the fear of that great mystery
the veiled woman, Isis,
mother, whom they fear to be greater than all else.

And I am sick unto death. Sick,
I say, sick. We live in a world where men have forgotten their
    offices
only taking the woman
        like good debaters
        assigned to the positive side
        on whom rests the burden of
        proof
only taking her on the surface—
she, I, we, can peel off layer after layer where you
have taken her and yet find the bottom deep and tight and
    untouched
and longing for the greater measure.

She, no it was I, walked with the moon in Pisces,
and felt the trout slipping down into the ocean.
The carved ice eagle of that party
was melting
into the gin and strawberries.
In its beak
someone had placed an American flag.
I found it hard to believe myself in this slippery unreal
man-made country. Look, look, look

I want to say; the eagle is a powerful bird.
In your fear, all you can do is carve him out of ice.
And that leaves only one alternative
in this temperate climate.
The ice eagle can do nothing
but melt.

1964

Reaching Out with the Hands of the Sun

And thereupon
That beautiful mild woman for whose sake
There's many a one shall find out all heartache
On finding that her voice is sweet & low
Replied: "To be born woman is to know—
Although they do not talk of it at school—
That we must labour to be beautiful."
        "Adam's Curse," W. B. Yeats

Atun-Re
the sun disk
whose rays end in hands
shines above us in New York
California
Egypt
sometimes even Alaska.
Walking across the desert,
he puts his scorching hands over our eyes
and turns vision into sounds,
waves
as the ocean,
drawing the pupils away from rattlesnakes & blurring
the hawks
that sail so unconcerned with heat
above our heads;
when we ride across the snow
and shaggy trees of Alaska
the sun's many hands
rub thick bear skins & tallow against the apples of our faces;
when we float down the river
without barks of gold or flutes or beautiful boys in the heavy
linen sails,
the sun's hands reach into the Nile
and pull out a glimmering eel
or a water lily,

holding it against the banks,
motioning for us to expect life anywhere,
even though it's not at once seen;
the hands coming from the rays of that disk
hold oranges, dates, figs, nuts
all those sweetmeats
that give a woman fat thighs
and a puffy face.

What am I to believe in this world?
The whirling sun disk
that speeds years away
puts out such rays with hands attached to each
that fling me one day against
the rough edges of mountains,
one day caress me, push me against the long mustaches I love;
my face varies from plain to dignified;
my figure from straight to plump;
my eyes from bright to small & sad;
my mouth, always a straight line—as if crossing a "t"
and I see the world change around me;
only one thing never changes.

Men remember,
love,
cherish,
beautiful women,
        as I've said,
        like April snow
like silk that rustles in a fragrant chest,
like a machine dripping with oil and running smoothly.

I am pooh-poohed
every time I say it.
        "a woman of your intelligence,"
            etc., etc.,
believing

such a superficial thing. "Only the
foolish
misguided,
the men with no balls,
or the ones that don't really matter,"
love a woman for her beauty
her physical self.
But I know different.
I've ruled;
I've walked with the mask of a falcon,
perhaps Horus
over my head,
walked everywhere, stiff & disguised,
walked in stone watching
the life around me,
the loving,
and not loving,
without sounds to interrupt or change history.
I've watched and know
that even the poets
whose blood is most filled with sun's light
and whose hands are wet
coming out of the rays of the moon,
love beautiful women,
writhe, turn,
upset their lives, leave their good wives,
when one walks by. And we,
with fat thighs,
or small breasts,
or thin delicate hair,
pale faces,
small eyes,
with only our elegant, small-wristed hands
to defend us
trying to catch one of the hands
on a ray from the sun,
loving our men faithfully

and with hope—
surely we deserve something more than platitudes.
We are the ones who know
    beauty is only skin deep.
But we also know
we would trade every ruby
stuffing and jamming our wealthy opulent hearts;
would trade every silver whistle
that alerts our brain,
keeps us sensitive and graceful to the world;
would trade every
miracle
inside our plain & ugly blood factories,
these bodies that never
serve us well,
for some beauty
they could recognize;
that would make the men stop
turn their heads,
twist their minds & lives around
for us/
for those of us who love them
and who never stop.
Whose hands are always radiating
out
ready to touch
the men
with fire
direct from the solar disk
who
brood
are dark often
with hands that come from the
unseen side
of the moon.

1969

Sometimes Even My Knees Smile

for Shep, at 21st birthday

You have replaced Beethoven
in my life.

My bones are piled up in neat little
stacks
waiting for you to put them in your pocket.

The prickly movement under my skin,
an alligator stranded on the desert,
is your mustache
which I have been stealing, hair by hair, in your
sleep each night.

A brown thrasher is pecking at my throat.
The breath of birds
that passes over my wrists and nipples
opening the umbrella,
is your touching. I would open up anything,
even my belly or crack open my bones
for you.

I would give you
anything
except a poem. Those I hold close
like diamonds up the ass in an African mine;
even those I would
give too
if you asked
but it is Beethoven you replaced
in my life.
And he had music so loud in his head
he didn't need words.

The poet is the lover who can't speak to—
isn't heard by—
his love.

1965

Love Passes Beyond the Incredible Hawk of Innocence

to S.S.

> The stairs will forget your footsteps;
> the rain will wash away all the invisible
> spots where you've stood;
> my hair will not curl in the places
> you've touched it;
> & newspapers will be printed each day
> mentioning neither of our names.

I had passed through the spinal doors
of 2 hospitals,
breathing ether
and passing clots of blood like
> soft-backed
> red-black
> beetles,
> each as large as a thumb.
I had eaten the bones of children
and washed dishes for the world.
I had lived in jails,
> the bars made of clocks striking 9 to 6
> with overtime on Saturdays;
> prison jobs stacking paper over my head
> filled with complaints,
> irritating as a dog locked up in a room and constantly
>   barking,
> each piece of paper/thousands a day/
> had to be individually smiled to
> till the weight fell down at night
> and the smiles crumbled like dry crusts of bread.
I had stood up to the insults of
national enemies,
> junior high school principals
> and assistant principals

who lived their lives by 24 lesson plans a week
                aim
                motivation
                pivotal questions
                procedures
                summaries
and retarded my own heartbeats with the
                frustration
                of retarded readers.
I had fallen in love with the sharp edges of razor blades
that will cut the flesh of your arms so fast you don't feel any
        pain.
I had signed my name in blood
in a thousand registers
and found that people laughed at my penmanship,
or criticized its execution.
I had spent years in alchemical experiments,
and only singed my hands
until they looked like a winter poplar at dusk.

But it was not until I met you,
my husband for two short years,
whose love was like the full moon on a night of total eclipse,
whose mind was like a flash flood,
whose eyes were like the sound of coyotes in the Southern
        California
hills 20 years ago,
whose words were a fire escape in a burning building,
whose boldness lifted me as a hawk would a snake
                before he flings it
                down on the ground
                to bash the life out of it,
whose madness captured me
        in the collapsing tunnel of my own defenses;
that world that had bled me,
                jailed me,
                starved me,

laughed at me,
rejected me,
was one I could feel
at last
getting at me,
as you might feel the
hot smokey air from
a burning room creeping under the door crack
in the room where you've been defending yourself;
it was not until I met you
that the door broke down
          —or I opened it—
and my innocence was consumed,
burned away.
Those of you who are listening to me now,
some walk leaving your prints in snow,
or soot from burning buildings,
some in jade from the stylized places you travel,
or ink that you've spilled in keeping accounts,
you know, I cannot doubt,
how indefinable the borders of countries are,
how easy to walk and find yourself having been in two countries
      or
two states, sometimes one foot in one,
the other foot in another.
You know how the worst ravages of childhood
in some ways never touch you,
while a feather or a leaf falling by chance as you walk on the
      street
at a later time, may bruise you
break your arm,
or destroy your life.
When we are innocent,
we know nothing about innocence,
live everything the hard way.
And it protects us.
It seemed to me as if I had been through all the possible

terrors; and meeting this one man
would relieve them all.
But that leaf, that feather,
something
must have pushed down my door.
No longer did the crystal pane surround me.
No longer could it protect me.
No longer could I walk in those same
impossible places
without realizing
their danger.

And that is the secret
        —if the word could be used to mean
                reason
                formula
                explanation
of why I can't have you
in my life
anymore,
why I can't dream of you like a sunset
        wringing out over the hills & a face
        reds, golds
        purples,
why I can't even desire you
or credit you with the magnificent passion you have.

You hurt me.
You locked me in a room and took away my glasses when you
        found me
reading a book by a man you hated;
you pounded my head against the floor when I wouldn't change
        my name;
you tried to lock me away in a mental institution when I wanted
        to
go to a writers' conference for two weeks,
you called up my old friends and said you'd castrate them if they

100

talked to me;
you hit me in the mouth every time I disagreed with you;
you would not let me answer the phone or open my own mail;
you threw out poems & letters that were from or about other
        men;
you created enormous debts and ridiculed me for worrying about
        them;
you made me feel guilty about everything in a way even an evil
        parent
could not have been able;
you hurt me,
and each time I wondered,
"What have I done wrong this time?"
And as long as I retained my innocence,
I believed I needed you,
felt I wanted you,
could not,
would not,
terminate the madness;
it was you,
in fact,
who had to do that,
sent me away
& knew it was final.

I have reached the age of 30.
but feel each moment of my life
has been clawed out
as if I were making a hole around
myself,
in which I could breathe.
Every breath has been labored for.
Every freedom paid for once & again.
But suffering protects people.
Keeps them involved in the situation at hand.
Does not allow the mind to wander
or become cynical.

Innocence is suffering,
and the loss of that innocence is something to fear.
But the poem can take its place
in this world.

                            Jewels dropped on the stairs
                            or growing on bushes & trees
                            remind me of your unreality.
                            The ivory-braceleted hand
                            picking up a pomegranate
                            which when opened
                            gleams,
                            with its rows of translucent seeds,
                            ready to be transplanted,
                            as a new kind of heart.
                            This could be my different life.
                            The faces on letters which bite at my
                                  fingers
                            when I tear the paper
                            and read out words, hard as green walnuts,
                            that would stain my fingers if I could
                                touch them
                            are your voice
                            which left such stains, long & streaked
                                across
                            my face.
                            The lesson of innocence:
                            that love is not inevitable
                            but must, like other good things
                            be chosen
                            to make any sense.

Not only the stairs
but my ears, muffling as soft towels,
will forget your footsteps.
The only traces rain will not wash away
are the jade prints left in Chinese poems.
Old hair falls out of old follicles

and more grows in.
The newspaper is not the poem
of our time.
Remember the walls of hospitals.
Every flower is a diary.
A mountain is a history; our bones
may constitute,
if we're lucky,
an interesting story.
Love passes over innocence,
beyond the incredible hawk which is the world
ready to tear us apart,
teaches us the meaning of something
once it is past.

1967

There's Plenty of Anguish at the Railroad

No, I don't know what your connection with the railroads is,
though you tell me it's father
who walked like a grizzly bear down the aisles
into a clubcar;
and he owned a branch that went from the dream waters of the
California coast to the Truth City ringed by rusty scissors.
But a ride on the train
takes me into
my own tunnel:
my own vision. How could I miss my own relatives,
yet there you were,
Mr. Twin, my brother, with water pouring from your hair and
streaming to the floor where your skinny double A feet rested
and the railroad passengers
who knew you
because
as you say
your slick father with his onyx ring
owned that branch,

well, they just wondered what you were doing,
wet, just out of the water,

and they didn't know me. I said, "I'm his sister
and it is also my relative who owns this branch of the train."

But family stuff is boring,
so it quickly vanished.
           Dance steps: one conch shell
                    one old sun
                    one peach
                    one sparkled baton
                    one, one, one;
                    one and one;
                    one and one;

and one;
and one;
and one;
and one and two;
and one and two;
Now that we have danced together on the train,
take out the sunflowers that
grow in your heart,
out from the juicy red meat. If you
don't practice taking them out,
they get stuck and then you can
never take them out. So
you do take them out, and instead of growing by the tracks,
as the train roars by,
you find
you have laid them on the tracks like Mary Pickford,
and they yell, "help, help,"
but your family train comes puffing by at 80 and
swoosh they are run over; then
        I have news for you
            since we danced together
                I don't want to go to bed with you anymore.
                    And it's not just because you're a relative
                        but it's because you're not blond
                            and look too much like my brother.

I still don't really know what your connection with trains is
even though you tell me time and again
I still can never see you travelling other than in a jet,
speeding across the ocean, and at some point,
nosing swiftly, somewhat mysteriously,
into
the sea.

1964

Exorcism

for my mother & a man who reminds me of her

get out.
stop dragging your feet through my veins
stop tripping over the flowerpots full of Heartsease at my elbow
stop sitting and sighing in my living room.
I live there.
stop mumbling your answers
stop hanging around with nothing to say
stop leaving your door open all the time
stop hanging on
give up. die. let yourself be pulled through the fire
if you come out of it
you will know how it really is to die
and how then
to be passionate for life
how to be hungry to move
to never stand still
to speak without mumbling
You exist by my pity
You want to remind me that you don't have what you want
You wait, hoping that I will give you some answers
will melt away your panic about life,
will put my energy in you to keep you going,
will reassure you that you are noble for suffering.
But I will not.
I will shake you angrily to make you see movement.
I will shout at you to hurt your eardrums and make you
     remember
pain, the first sensation of living,
I will slam your sloppy open door and scold you for your messy
     habits
I will wake you up when you want to sleep, typing or playing
     music
and I will ignore you when you want to be awake

I will find love defiantly to show you it exists only when you are
not pining.
I will point to my scars constantly and remind you that they are
what wake me up and renew my desire to live.
I will wish and pine and long for my own goals but show you
those feelings are only beautiful when backed up by spunk and
    willpower
and the drive and energy to explore everywhere,
to look for beauty in each motion.
And I will even endure you,
will not send you away from my house,
will try to find some beauty in your ridiculous life.
Will not throw you out in the world
as you deserve to be,
you slug who crawls on my damp sidewalks without even a shell,
you broken jellyfish who gives swimmers a rash,
you poor sad poet with nothing to say
without even the energy to lead your own life with any style.

1969

The Magellanic Clouds

(*for Eleanor who likes to see her name in print*)

The photographic plate is blurred.
That blurry area
is where you laughed and
breathed on the plate; lizard skinned
prickly pears roll out of your mouth; a purple bird
twists your tongue with his beak
and crazy cactus leaves of love pin you luckily to
one man;
you have a mouthful of stars when you laugh
and you fall over the milky way at your feet.
Next door the Magellanic Clouds swirl
and try to force themselves into your paintings
but you are too happy painting
little hearts and big hearts and sticking them
all over your husband
who is a river washing silver fish over you in the dark.

Look carefully.
My scream makes a silver line on the graph.
The photographic plate is blurred.
That blurry area
is the Magellanic Clouds
from another galaxy.
Inside me swirls something like the Magellanic
Clouds.
All the animals I ride are found in the Magellanic Clouds.
My life is destined to be a cloud,
galaxies, light years,
removed. The dust storm on the desert. The fog over the river.
A handful of dust with tiny shell fragments.
A gold outline against the sky.

How can I explain it to you and all the succulent women I know.
Wives, mothers, loved, protected,
by men they love,
having the shoulder to curl their heads into at night.
How can I explain to myself this dust cloud that is my life?
I talk in my sleep, just as I talk when I'm awake.
No one listens to me but strangers.
Once a blue vein of electricity came to me in the Magellanic
     Clouds
and said there is a price
on everyone's life.
Uncurling my ears like new leaves,
I looked at my world,
my scarred body,
my missing children,
separation from the men who spoke my language.
The price is to walk
alone
up the stairs,
alone
every night with your candle,
and alone
down the stairs
alone
every morning with white footsteps
and teacups of tears.
In your daydreams you must carry the bodies of your children
wrapped in white and strapped to stiff boards;
people will chase you and accuse you of murder.
The children will sing in your ears and cut you with the
sharp corners of their smiles.
Your songs will be bled out
of you
every day, as you are cut with different tools,
razor blades, knives, scissors, grass, paper, glass.
One day the words will come out of your elbows and one day

out of your knees. Scars and holes and craters will cover you.
When people look at you they will run away
but words,
the words you've bought will creep out of holes
like beautiful skeins of thread.
Some day I will vanish in the Magellanic Clouds
but will wait in rooms to get inside of paintings.
Even the electricity, the fire
tells me I will
not have to spend all my
time
in the sky.
Someday it will be my breath blurring the photographic plates
and the astronomers will say
"See that cloudy spot on the plate?
We once thought it was the Magellanic Clouds, but they have
moved
farther out
into space.
It is something new, another enormous cloud made up of strange
gases and foreign particles. It is something new
and we have no name for it yet,"
and I will breathe harder,
will blow harder,
will blur more of the plate,
will pass through rooms and rooms and rooms of memories in the
    shape
of apples, birds, iron wheels.

The clouds, the clouds, the Magellanic Clouds, the clouds in my
heart, the clouds I ride on, the clouds under my bed,
the clouds in my life, the clouds always in
the next room seeping under the door.

I am a cloud,
dust on the desert,

fog over the waters,
gases in the sky,

Can there be any
sadness
once I am named.

1969

The Birds of Paradise Being Very Plain Birds

"What do they look like," he said.
I said, "They are very very plain,
until they ruffle their neck feathers."

This is a city where
beauty is
unexpected.

They threw the jaguar a dead rabbit,
whole, white, long ears still warm,
pink eye holes in his soft rabbit head;
feeding time at 3 p.m.,
the animals all waiting for their fresh meat;
the jaguar holding the rabbit in his thick paws,
started with the head, working a hole open until
he had the brains exposed, and he continued to lick,
eating at the red mass, until I heard the woman next to me
saying, "I suppose it's natural, but it's so horrible,"
and another saying, "Look how he's got the brains all at once,"
and I, having sat there a whole hour on the bench in the lion
    house
watching the families walking about
looking at all the great cats, the black leopard,
the lion with her two cubs, the two large jaguars,
felt myself dead and limp, felt myself the rabbit,
thrown into the cage, foolishly, Romantically,
having just before visited the monkey house and watched the
beautiful, dark, white-crested Diana monkies with their grey
    beards
neurotically run in circles about the cage, touching,
as in a ritual, a certain spot on the wall each time around,
and thinking how cage life drove an animal into mazes of himself,
his cage mates chosen for him, his life circumscribed and focused
on eating, his play watched by it-doesn't-matter-whom, just
watched, always watched. I felt myself there too,

maudlin and sentimental, I felt myself in each place—
the lonesome panda, Chi-Chi,
picking at her foot, soft dirty fur,
alone, sitting aimlessly picking at her foot,
the sea-lion from 40 degrees of latitude trying to get some sun
        here at
50 degrees of latitude
the buddha mountain goat staring out from the
rocks,
the mountains
that weren't even above sea-level;

curiously,
you felt the desperation of the jaguar
in the cage
who had nothing to divert him,
no steaming jungle path,
no trees to crouch in,
no brush to stalk through,
no deer at the water hole to watch,
no bell bird to ring through the night, as he changed the colors of
his eyes,
who had not even a live rabbit to chase, nor anywhere to chase it,
but dead, fresh-dead, rabbit, thrown to him, limp,
easy to lick the steaming brains from . . .

A different sun shines on this place,
colder perhaps from a different direction,
like a lemon in a glass pretending it gives light,
a sun that dashes all hope of relationship with the hot sun,
continues his chilly breath,
a sun I might find unrolling itself as a ball of wool,
when I look up into the sky for it.
A sun that might stand behind the pillar of the house next door,
rather than say hello to me as I pass by,
a shy neighbor, you might say,
but really a different sun,

not the one composed of flaming gases I read about in
astronomy books.
"Look at that hearse with the yellow flowers on it," she said,
but her friends on the bus did not see what she saw,
and she looked again, to find a beige colored truck with sacks of
potatoes on its roof. It happens all the time, I told her,
some of us have bad vision, are crippled, have defects, and
our reality is a different one, not the
correct and ascertainable one,
and sometimes it makes us dotty and lonely
but also it makes us poets.
Some people take drugs to change their ascertainable vision
into this cracking one, and we look at the honeycomb floor
and wonder why the head always aches, the belly always
holds a bit of nausea.
We know where the reality is, don't we?

That always causes a long pause.

"Look at that truck with all those sacks of potatoes," she said,
but her friends in the limousine did not know what she was
         saying,
she was out of her senses, perhaps with grief,
the hearse with the yellow flowers on it travelling too slowly in
the sunlight, the day too slow, too still, the day
when everyone's vision cracked a bit with the sun,
the strain of the bird flying through the window,
the Bird of Paradise suddenly ruffling his feathers,
a change to beauty.

The buddha-goat, big-horned mountain sheep,
sitting staring—one could imagine his eyes as blue
as yours. What does a mountain goat with false mountains
in a city zoo think,
sitting all day, not moving. What do you
think, staring at this expensive ugly wallpaper,
sitting still, in this city, not talking,

the Buddha-Shepherd,
a sheep in his fake mountains.
Eyes so blue.

A dream: lungs.
Lying on the plate with thick crockery the delicate lungs
heaving with unvacated breath,
the jaguar walking around the table
and the Buddha-sheep sitting above, outside
the window, outside the mountain,
staring at the lungs, struggling fish . . .

A patient dying of cancer will have
lost the sensation of pain in many parts of the body.
Smoking a cigarette
he may not notice it burning through his fingers.
Sitting on a blade, he might not feel it slice his body in half.
Tenderness for the oblivion the Buddha needs,
someone to understand that he has faced all of space and eternity;
it riddles him with pockets and cell-groups of infinity, and does he
feel what is happening now? He stares past himself,
ignoring me.
He says the ear is no good here, neither
is the eye. False mountains
the habitat a dream.

No Birds of Paradise, he also tells me
in other zoos he's seen. What do they look like?
Each has a different look, I say,
but all plain,
very plain, until that ruffling starts.

Once again he is the Buddha sheep,
staring past me into the mirror, his wisdom, mazes of himself,
I the rabbit, never having run in the fields or stolen carrots from
Farmer Brown, raised in a cage,
bred for food,

crouching especially timid but not moving,
the day the keepers came in to wring necks, the hunt never
     starting,
having been already over at the start
      —the brains go first,
      a hungry animal licking his way down,
      through the red mass,
      no longer a brain.

The Birds of Paradise have only an occasional
and unpredictable
beauty.

c. 1966

The Buddha Inherits 6 Cars on His Birthday

I. THE RED CAR

I believe it was out of the red one that George Washington
    stepped,
or someone who looked like G.W.
The corridor was made of fibrous blood
and his feet sank in darkly
as teeth into a pear. Going past the service desk
he was paged by a man who had sitting in front of him a
tall jelly glass holding his false teeth. The gums,
false pink.
G.W. was in no mood for dalliance.
"Send all the seamstresses up at once," he said,
and when they got there he undressed them all,
picked the most voluptuous one
and gave her some cloth to
sew.

II. THE BLUE CAR

It smelled like new rubber inside.
The man who drove it had no imagination.
"Will I turn into a machine," he thought,
but no
in a few days they found
a desert rat driving that new blue Ford.
And it seemed peculiar
but it's easier not to question things
these days.

III. THE GREEN CAR

Emily and James stepped out of their green car.
It was made of old metal melted down.
In your Lee corduroy dungarees and sweatshirt you
look so handsome.
I'm not particular

as long as you have money and style.
This money is easy to spend,
but if you tried to stuff dollar bills inside me you'd find
a yawning gap, hole
at the bottom where everything falls out
Oh pity
there is such an empty space
Oh pity
that the lives of some of us are
so vain.

IV. THE YELLOW CAR

A very small man met a very large woman.
They were both in the teen-age section of the library.
They discovered they both liked the Mona Lisa. They
discovered they both listened to the 1812 Overture.
When true love comes,
               hallelujah
                      you know it!

V. THE TWO-TONE CAR

There are fish that change color for camouflage, but it is a fact that
blind ones never do. Experimentation follows it up. Scientists painted
a tank black at one end and white at the other. It was observed that
a certain fish would become grey as he got just in the middle at the
dividing line. This was the only time he showed up as a different color
from his surroudings, either black or white. Apparently, he could not
make an instantaneous change. At the dividing line he always turned
grey.

VI. OLD CARS

In my car of crocodile teeth, in my
car of old candle wax, in
my car of tiger paws padding the waspy dust, in my car of
cat's teeth crushing the brittle insect wings, in my
car of leather straps, in my car of folded paper, silvery and pink,
in my car of Alpine tents, in my car of bits & braces,

in my car of fishing line, in my car at the bottom of a
violin, in my car as small as a flea hopping on the dog,
in my own car I want to drive
everywhere
every place there is to go.

c. 1968

The Universes

*For you I would build a whole new
universe around myself. This
isn't shit it is poetry.*
                              Jack Spicer

FIRST UNIVERSE

Walking on this springy grass
which grows
like separate bunches of yarrow
on the dunes at the beach
this meadow
surrounded by trees just dotting themselves
with new flowers,
a little like blood
spotting the handkerchief
the coughing winds

the shepherd in this meadow is you.
Your hair curling up
as the green buds of leaves are
on those trees
and you are here because the sheep
are fat and woolly
and you want something dumb
to love,
to be near

but I have buried myself in the wool of the fattest
sheep, the skin furrowed almost bubbled like the foam that comes
up on soup stock, as the bone boils, and is skimmed off.
This wool will be skimmed off too
when the weather's warmer.
Now I'm
here underneath it all

120

hoping you will come and hug this woolly creature
and hold me too
accidentally,
as I hover inside
this universe of wool,
of the soft skin under your eyes when you sleep
the thin ridges of your ear that remain cool,
of all the parts
of you I want to touch
of the reason I've followed you
hidden in the wool of the fattest sheep.

SECOND UNIVERSE

The London *Times* tells me that "Mr. Humphrey,
                              accompanied by
M. Pompidou, the French Prime Minister, was
taking part in a ceremony at the foot of
a statue of George Washington when a part
of the crowd started to shout, 'U.S.
assassins.' "
Now where does George Washington live?
and how?
and in what form?
and why have I called him the Father of My Country?
I think George Washington probably lives
in the U.S. Treasury Dept., where his picture is
on every dollar
bill and every silver quarter, which means
he's useful — like the telephone
and so I've devoted myself to his memory and image.
And it is quite probably true that as the symbol
of common currency
he is an assassin.
            We are told that an assassin was an oriental
            who was so charmed, enchanted, if you will, by
            the delights of eating and smoking hashish that he

121

would do anything for his master to perpetuate these
delights.

George Washington money.
What delights are supplied thereby?
and what we wouldn't do to preserve them.
This universe is one where each man fiercely possesses
his own name, his own individuality,
and will kill to keep it.
Now there are many just arguments against killing
but when it comes right down to the nitty gritty
most men will proudly take the title assassin if it means
defending what is their own.

This universe is one where I find you
at the foot of every possible statue
and even I have called you assassin, especially when you stood
under the statue of George Washington,
but only because I knew you could not love me if you killed
me. Love is for the Living.
A little smile, or nostalgia over the grave
is not love.
It writhes and struggles like a bucket of fishing worms
trying to remain separate, alive.

This universe costs nothing to get into.
Money is only a symbol here,
I loving the picture of George Washington on the dollar,
the quarter.

This universe is for love and its assassins.

THIRD UNIVERSE

A little white gibbon, with arms like palm branches
is lying by a concrete ditch of water.
She seems to be looking at a nut someone has given her

or is it a ring
with a stone as green
as a lizard slipping down the drain
of a metal washtub.
The gibbon's fur is white, soft,
her toes, delicate like yours. The ring
takes her where I'd like to go:
a place where the poem
is part of the oil in her skin;
if I were there I could touch you whenever I wanted to.
You might hold me against the cold sun in my tongue.
It is, of course, an enchanted ring.
The little white gibbon found it
because it was there.
Doesn't that explain most everything in this particular
universe? Even the curling hair, the soft cheek,
the kiss that isn't given?
Or the one that is.

FOURTH UNIVERSE

All my universes are the same.
You know it.
They would all have someone like you in them,
and of course me.
That might make us travellers in space,
not an improbable occurrence
since I would travel anywhere to find you,
and sometimes it would seem you'd travel anywhere to
leave me.
What happens when two
zen masters get together?

Answer: they have tea.

Oh please remember how soft my small breasts are,
like kittens who've just opened their eyes;

remember my own clear grey eyes,
that look past all the rubble, past the prepossessing body
and very bluest eyes, into a strange animal,
your soul, a Platonist would say,
a duck quacking down the river, not anything like those dead
bloody heads I saw in the poultry shop window.

What happens when two zen students get together?

Answer: one becomes master
or one goes away,
but only after great troubles.
And they never have their tea.

FIFTH UNIVERSE

the bare thin
branches
coming out of the fog
like a little girl's pigtails flying in the wind
or all the little hairs in your nose, magnified a million times.
An image in sepia tones
of you, as a gangster with a tommy gun,
brass knuckles, and of course a carnation in your buttonhole.
What other incongruities
does this world present?
Your dashing clothes and authority on the phone,
yet those baby fingers, with nails like small half circles
sometimes found left in the paper-hole puncher,
nails bitten down to the quick,
small fingers,
a grubby child's hand,
a grubby child's soul bundled in all that continental manner.

The fog in this world slips into my own knuckles and joints,
giving me aches; somehow the arteries in my heart feel
knotted also, my whole body a cave of fog—

124

that must be what frightened you so, or disgusted you.
Yes, even in my imaginary universes I find you
walking away from me and feel my tongue dry in my mouth
a dead snail, curled up, its shell
traced with strange patterns the fat living body
had made. Everything I say is a shell
for what I feel.
And of course I feel myself more and more a shell.

Words and words and words.
Your foot on the chromium bumper of a 1937 Buick,
the year I was born.
Words mean nothing if there is not a life to back them up.
Are you such a gangster,
or are those only images too,
more words?

I would see you every day of my life
and in fact I do.
Whether you're there or not: I see the shepherd
in one world, the assassin hiding under George Washington's
    statue
in another, the Zen master hitting me over the head as an
answer to my koan,
the gangster,
the naughty child.

In the words of the lion-poet, "For you I would build a whole
new universe around myself."
But you should in fact
be a little frightened of it.
You are
in it
anything that I choose
to make you.

1966

The Pink Dress

I could not wear that pink dress tonight.
The velvet one
lace tinting the cuffs with all
the coffee
of longing. My bare shoulder
slipping whiter
than foam
out of the night to remind me
of my own
vulnerability.

I could not wear that pink dress tonight
because it is a dress
that slips memories like
the hands
of obscene strangers
all over my body.
And in my fatigue I could not fight away the images
and their mean touching.

I couldn't wear that pink dress,
the velvet one you had made for me,
all year, you know.

I thought I would tonight because
once again
you have let me enter your house
and look at myself
some mornings
in your mirrors.
                    But
I could not wear that pink dress tonight
because it reminded me
of everything
that hurts.

It reminded me of a whole year
during which
I wandered,
a gypsy,
and could not come into your house.
It reminded me of the picture of a blond girl
you took with you to Vermont
and shared your woods with.
The pretty face you left over your bed to stare
at me
and remind me
each night
that you preferred her face to mine,
and which you left there to stare at me
even when you saw how it
broke me,
my calm,
like a stick smashing across my own
plain, lonesome face,
and a face which you only
took down
from your wall
after I had mutilated it
and pushed pins in it to get those smug
smiling eyes off my cold
winter
body.

I couldn't wear that pink dress tonight
because it reminded me
of the girl who made it,
whom you slept with
last year while I was sitting in hotel rooms
wondering why I had to live
with a face
so stony no man could love it.

I could not wear that pink dress
because it reminded me
of how I camp on your doorstep now,
still a gypsy,
still a colorful imaginative beggar
in my pink dress,
building a fire in the landowner's
woods, and my own fierceness
that deserts me
when a man
no, when you,
show a little care and concern
for my presence.

I could not wear that pink dress tonight.
It betrayed all that was strong in me.
The leather boots I wear to stomp through the world
and remind everyone
of the silver and gold and diamonds
from fairy tales
glittering in their lives.
And of the heavy responsibility
we all must bear
just being so joyfully alive
just letting the blood take its own course
in intact vessels
in veins.
That pink dress betrayed my one favorite image
—the motorcyclist riding along the highway
independent
alone
exhilarated with movement
a blackbird
more beautiful than any white ones.

But I went off
not wearing the pink dress,

thinking how much I love you
and how if a woman loves a man who does not love her,
it is, as some good poet said,
a pain in the ass.
For both of them.

I went off thinking about all the girls
you preferred to me.
Leaving behind that dress,
remembering one of the colors
of pain
Remembering that my needs
affront you,
my face is not beautiful to you;
you would not share your woods with me.

And the irony
of my images.
That you are the motorcycle rider.
Not I.
I am perhaps,
at best,
the pink dress
thrown against the back
of the chair.
The dress I could not wear
tonight.

c. 1970

The Mechanic

to T.W.

Most men use
their eyes
like metronomes
clicking off the beats
of a woman's walk;
how her hips press
against the cloth, as figs just before
they split their purple skins
on the tree,
measuring how much of her walk
goes into bed at night,
the jar of the sky
being filled with the Milky Way
glittering for every time
she moves her lips

but of course
the secrets
are not the obvious beats
in the song
that even a bad drummer can play

hearing the speed of the motor
—it too made up of beats—
so fast,
subtle, I suppose,
they register
as continuous sound
or the heart which of course
beats without any fan belt to keep it
cool.

it is a test,
a rhythm,
they could not see
with those measuring eyes
though perhaps there are some
whose fingers and ears
are so close to the motors
with clean oil passing through their ears
and draining properly into the brain pan,
perhaps a few . . .

who can tell
what the secret bleeding of a woman
is all about

As a woman
with oily stars sticking
on all the tip points
of my skin
I could never
trust a man
who wasn't a mechanic,
a man who uses his
eyes,
his hands,
listens to
the
heart.

1966

With Words

for Tony

Poems come from incomplete knowledge.
From the sense of seeing
an unfinished steel bridge
that you'd like to walk across,
your imaginary footprints floating like pieces
of paper,
where the metal ends,
on the cold water
far below;
or the moon disappearing
behind a cloud
just when you could almost
see the face
of the man standing next
to you
in the olive trees;

And consequently,
I write about those
whose hands
I've touched once,
trying to remember
which fingers had the rings
on them,
speculating from a few words
what the dialogue of a lifetime
would have been,
making the facts up
out of the clouds of breath we release
on a winter night.
How can I
then
make a poem for you?

whose skillful hands
could make expert
blueprints
of all my bones?
There is no need
for a bridge between us;
we sleep on the same side of the bed.
Your mustache.
inherited from some stealthy Cossack
who kissed your great-great-great-
grandmother
and slid his icy cock between her warm
legs one night
is no mystery
to me.
I can relive
its history,
drawing lines all over my body.
I have no questions
either
about your powerful legs,
arms,
back,
or the quick mind
which leads the body around on a leash.

Forgive me then,
if the poems I write
are about the fragments,
the broken bridges,
and unlit fences
in my life.
For the poet,
the poem
is not
the measure
of his love. It is

the measure
of all he's lost, or
never seen,
or what has no life,
unless he gives it life
with words.

c. 1968

I Have Had to Learn to Live With My Face

You see me alone tonight.
My face has betrayed me again,
   the garage mechanic who promises to fix my car
   and never does.

My face
that my friends tell me is so full of character;
my face
I have hated for so many years;
my face
I have made an angry contract to live with
though no one could love it;
my face that I wish you would bruise and batter
and destroy, napalm it, throw acid on it,
so that I might have another
or be rid of it at last.

I drag peacock feathers behind me
to erase the trail of the moon. Those tears
I shed for myself,
sometimes in anger.
There is no pretense in my life. The man who lives with me
must see something beautiful,

like a dark snake coming out of my mouth,
or love the tapestry of my actions, my life/this body, this
face, they have nothing to offer
but angry insistence, their presence.
I hate them,
want my life to be more.
Hate their shadow on even my words.
I sell my soul for good plumbing
and hot water,
            I tell everyone;
and my face is soft,

opal,
a feathering of snow
against the
        cold black leather coat
which is night.
         You,
         night,
         my face against the chilly
         expanse
         of your back.
Learning to live with what you're born with
is the process,
the involvement,
the making of a life.
And I have not learned happily
to live with my face,
that Diane which always looks better on film
than in life.
I sternly accept this plain face,
and hate every moment of that sternness.

I want to laugh at this ridiculous face
    of lemon rinds
    and vinegar cruets
    of unpaved roads
    and dusty file cabinets
    of the loneliness of Wall Street at night
    and the desert of school on a holiday
but I would have to laugh alone in a cold room
Prefer the anger
that at least for a moment gives me a proud profile.
Always, I've envied
    the rich
      the beautiful
     the talented
       the go-getters
        of the world. I've watched

myself
remain
alone
isolated
a fish that swam through the net
because I was too small
  but remained alone
  in deep water because the others were caught
  taken away
It is so painful for me to think now,
to talk about this; I want to go to sleep and never wake up.
The only warmth I ever feel is wool covers on a bed.
But self-pity could trail us all, drag us around on the bottom of
shoes like squashed snails so that
we might never fight/ and it is anger I want now, fury,
to direct at my face and its author,
to tell it how much I hate what it's done to me,
to contemptuously, sternly, brutally even, make it live with itself,
look at itself every day,
and remind itself
that reality is
learning to live with what you're born with,
noble to have been anything but defeated,
that pride and anger and silence will hold us above beauty,
though we bend down often with so much anguish for
a little beauty,
a word, like the blue night,
  the night of rings covering the floor and glinting
  into the fire, the water, the wet earth, the age of songs,
  guitars, angry busloads of etched tile faces, old gnarled
  tree trunks, anything with the beauty of wood, teak, lemon,
  cherry
I lost my children because I had no money, no husband,
I lost my husband because I was not beautiful,
I lost everything a woman needs, wants,
almost
before I became a woman,

137

my face shimmering and flat as the moon
with no features.

I look at pictures of myself as a child.
I looked lumpy, unformed, like a piece of dough,
and it has been my task as a human being
to carve out a mind, carve out a face,
carve out a shape with arms & legs, to put a voice inside,
and to make a person from a presence.
And I don't think I'm unique.
I think a thousand of you, at least, can look at those old photos,
reflect on your life
and see your own sculpture at work.

I have made my face as articulate as I can,
and it turns out to be a peculiar face with too much
bone in the bridge of the nose, small eyes, pale lashes,
thin lips, wide cheeks, a rocky chin,
But it's almost beautiful compared to the sodden mass of dough I
    started out with.

I wonder how we learn to live
with our faces?
They must hide so much pain,
so many deep trenches of blood,
so much that would terrorize and drive others away, if they
could see it. The struggle to control it
articulates the face.
And what about those people
with elegant noses and rich lips?

What do they spend their lives struggling for?

Am I wrong I constantly ask myself
to value the struggle
more than the results?

Or only to accept a beautiful face
if it has been toiled for?

Tonight I move alone in my face;
want to forgive all the men whom I've loved
who've betrayed me.
After all, the great betrayer is that one I carry around each day,
which I sleep with at night. My own face,
angry building I've fought to restore
imbued with arrogance, pride, anger and scorn.
To love this face
would be to love a desert mountain,
a killer, rocky, water hard to find, no trees anywhere/
perhaps I do not expect anyone
to be strange enough to love it;
but you.

c. 1969

Love Letter Postmarked Van Beethoven

for a man I love
more than I should,
intemperance being something
a poet cannot afford

I am too angry to sleep beside you,
you big loud symphony who fell asleep drunk;
I try to count sheep and instead
find myself counting the times I would like to shoot you
in the back,
your large body
with its mustaches that substitute for love
and its knowledge of motorcycle mechanics that substitutes
for loving me;
why aren't you interested in
my beautiful little engine?
It needs a tune-up tonight, dirty with the sludge of
anger, resentment,
and the pistons all sticky, the valves
afraid of the lapping you might do,
the way you would clean me out of your life.

I count the times your shoulders writhe
and you topple over
after I've shot you with my Thompson Contender
    (using the .38-caliber barrel
    or else the one they recommend for shooting rattlesnakes).
I shoot you each time in that wide dumb back,
insensitive to me,
glad for the mild recoil of the gun
that relieves a little of my repressed anger
each time I discharge a bullet into you;
one for my father who deserted me and whom you masquerade as,
every night, when you don't come home
or even telephone to give me an idea of when to expect you;

the anguish of expectation in one's life
and the hours when the mind won't work, waiting
for the sound of footsteps on the stairs,
the key turning in the lock;
another bullet for my first lover,
a boy of 18
	(but that was when I was 18 too)
who betrayed me and would not marry me.
You too, betrayer,
you who will not give me your name as even a token of affection;
another bullet,
and of course each time
the heavy sound of your body falling over in heavy shoes
a lumber jacket, and a notebook in which you write down
everything
but reality;
another bullet for those men
who said they loved me
and followed other women into their silky bedrooms
and kissed them behind curtains,
who offered toasts to other women,
making me feel ugly, undesirable;
anger, fury, the desire to cry or to shake you back
to the way you used to love me,
even wanted to,
knowing that I have no recourse,
that if I air my grievances you'll only punish me more
or tell me to leave,
and yet knowing that silent grievances
will erode my brain,
make pieces of my ability to love
fall off,
like fingers from a leprosied hand;
and I shoot another bullet into your back,
trying to get to sleep,
only wanting you to touch me with some gesture of affection;
this bullet for the bad husband who would drink late in bars

and not take me with him,
talking and flirting with other women,
and who would come home, without a friendly word, and sleep
celibate next to my hungry body;
a bullet for the hypocrites;
a bullet for my brother who could not love me without guilt;
a bullet for the man I love who never listens to me;
a bullet for the men who run my country without consulting me;
a bullet for the man who says I am a fool to expect anyone to
    listen to me;
a bullet for the man who wrote a love poem to me
and a year later threw it away, saying it was a bad poem.
If I were Beethoven, by now I'd have tried every
dissonant chord;
were I a good marksman, being paid to test this new Thompson
Contender, I'd have several dozen dead rattlers lying
along this path already;
instead, I am ashamed of my anger
at you
whom I love
whom I ask for so much more than you want to give.
A string quartet would be too difficult right now.
Let us have the first movement of the Moonlight Sonata
I will try counting the notes
instead of sheep.

c. 1969

Thanking My Mother for Piano Lessons

The relief of putting your fingers on the keyboard,
as if you were walking on the beach
and found a diamond
as big as a shoe;

as if
you had just built a wooden table
and the smell of sawdust was in the air,
your hands dry and woody;

as if
you had eluded
the man in the dark hat who had been following you
all week;

the relief
of putting your fingers on the keyboard,
playing the chords of
Beethoven,
Bach,
Chopin
      in an afternoon when I had no one to talk to,
      when the magazine advertisement forms of soft sweaters
      and clean shining Republican middle-class hair
      walked into carpeted houses
      and left me alone
      with bare floors and a few books

I want to thank my mother
for working every day
in a drab office
in garages and water companies
cutting the cream out of her coffee at 40
to lose weight, her heavy body
writing its delicate bookkeeper's ledgers

alone, with no man to look at her face,
her body, her prematurely white hair
in love
        I want to thank
my mother for working and always paying for
my piano lessons
before she paid the Bank of America loan
or bought the groceries
or had our old rattling Ford repaired.

I was a quiet child,
afraid of walking into a store alone,
afraid of the water,
the sun,
the dirty weeds in back yards,
afraid of my mother's bad breath,
and afraid of my father's occasional visits home,
knowing he would leave again;
afraid of not having any money,
afraid of my clumsy body,
that I knew
        no one would ever love

But I played my way
on the old upright piano
obtained for $10,
played my way through fear,
through ugliness,
through growing up in a world of dime-store purchases,
and a desire to love
a loveless world.

I played my way through an ugly face
and lonely afternoons, days, evenings, nights,
mornings even, empty
as a rusty coffee can,
played my way through the rustles of spring

and wanted everything around me to shimmer like the narrow tide
on a flat beach at sunset in Southern California,
I played my way through
an empty father's hat in my mother's closet
and a bed she slept on only one side of,
never wrinkling an inch of
the other side,
waiting,
waiting,

I played my way through honors in school,
the only place I could
talk
    the classroom,
    or at my piano lessons, Mrs. Hillhouse's canary always
    singing the most for my talents,
    as if I had thrown some part of my body away upon entering
    her house
    and was now searching every ivory case
    of the keyboard, slipping my fingers over black
    ridges and around smooth rocks,
    wondering where I had lost my bloody organs,
    or my mouth which sometimes opened
    like a California poppy,
    wide and with contrasts
    beautiful in sweeping fields,
    entirely closed morning and night,

I played my way from age to age,
but they all seemed ageless
or perhaps always
old and lonely,
wanting only one thing, surrounded by the dusty bitter-smelling
leaves of orange trees,
wanting only to be touched by a man who loved me,
who would be there every night
to put his large strong hand over my shoulder,

whose hips I would wake up against in the morning,
whose mustaches might brush a face asleep,
dreaming of pianos that made the sound of Mozart
and Schubert without demanding
that life suck everything
out of you each day,
without demanding the emptiness
of a timid little life.

I want to thank my mother
for letting me wake her up sometimes at 6 in the morning
when I practiced my lessons
and for making sure I had a piano
to lay my school books down on, every afternoon.
I haven't touched the piano in 10 years,
perhaps in fear that what little love I've been able to
pick, like lint, out of the corners of pockets,
will get lost,
slide away,
into the terribly empty cavern of me
if I ever open it all the way up again.
Love is a man
with a mustache
gently holding me every night,
always being there when I need to touch him;
he could not know the painfully loud
music from the past that
his loving stops from pounding, banging,
battering through my brain,
which does its best to destroy the precarious gray matter when I
am alone;
he does not hear Mrs. Hillhouse's canary singing for me,
liking the sound of my lesson this week,
telling me,
confirming what my teacher says,
that I have a gift for the piano
few of her other pupils had.

When I touch the man
I love,
I want to thank my mother for giving me
piano lessons
all those years,
keeping the memory of Beethoven,
a deaf tortured man,
in mind;
        of the beauty that can come
from even an ugly
past.

1970

My Trouble

my trouble
is that I have the spirit of Gertrude Stein
but the personality of Alice B. Toklas;
craggy, grand
stony ideas
but
all I can do
is embroider Picasso's drawings
and bake hashish fudge.
I am poor
and don't have very much to say
am usually taken for
somebody's
secretary.

c. 1971

Steely Silence

If a man calls himself a poet
(and many do)
he is expected to charm you
with his speech.
Yet the time for speaking
is best
a formal time
and speech best
when prepared / for a purpose.
Dinner time is for eating
and afternoon for reading.
Night for sleep and love.
Most talk is simple communicaton
      "Pass the butter."
      "How do you get to the post office?"
      "What is your name?"
Yet talk is often created
where none need be.

Forgive me.
I have no light conversation.
Forgive me,
I have no literary or witty remarks.
My nature is dark
I am heavy to walk with
and silent in the company of friends.
I am limited to the subjects
most people don't care to discuss.
My tongue is my weapon.
I only use it
in moments of danger.
Forgive me then, for my silence.

It is a sign of trust.

1972

Smudging

Smudging is the term using for lighting small oil fires in the orange groves at night when the temperatures are too low, to keep the leaves and fruit warm, so as not to lose the crop.

I come out of a California orange grove
the way a meteor might be
plucked out of an Arizona desert. The icy origins
of genes
could easily be
flaming ones
          And in my head
those red-hot rocks
shake down into a bed of
coals, oranges roll off the shelves,
amber sticks on the roof of my mouth,
honey glistens in glass jars, the combs full of music,
—all in the back of my head/ the gold
of the small loops in my ears
is the sound of a king cobra crossing the rocks,
tigers walk across my lips/ the gold is
in my head. It is the honeysuckle of an island.
This gold is in your house;
I sleep in your bed at night
and love you,
          but the firelight from those smudging pots flickers
against my eyes, burned by the eclipse this year,
and reminds me:
                    When I was five years old, we lived on the
                    edge of Orange County, in an orange grove,
                    in a small two room house with a sagging
                    screened porch. Outside the kitchen at
                    night when it was near frosting, the
                    immigrant laborers would build fires in the
                    smudge pots to keep the trees from freezing.
                    The poetry of dew-points would be on the

news each night, and after we went to bed,
the flickering of these fires would embroider
the windows, and the sounds of voices
talking in Spanish and laughing over their
tequila bottles would wander into the
windows like turning lawn sprinklers.
Our doors had locks that opened with
skeleton keys. You could purchase them in
dime stores. The flimsy jambs and lintels
could have been pushed down by children, and
my mother was not at all secure in her
plain whiteness. Those voices frightened
her. My father was never home. I was a
child with a father who was a sailor, a
child who did not even know what a fishing
rod looked like. My mother stood up in
agony, all night, in the dark, every night
there was smudging and the Chicanos were
sitting on our steps laughing, drinking, or
under the kitchen window, talking.
Orange groves in California
are the boundaries
of my childhood.
Nights
        when the temperatures hovered
near the mouth of frost
on the thermometer/
pots of glowing oil
tended by dark Mexicans
on dark nights
in the dark rows of the dark-leaved trees. Each orange shining
like a cold sour gold anger
on the bushy tough arms
of the tree.
                I remember those hard knots
of light
that turned into the fruit

for dew-soaked breakfasts.
But it was the smudge pots
burning
like old lamps in a dim room,
warming the trees
glowing in the orchards
as I passed on asphalt highways
unable to talk
that reminded me
of my own unripe sour tight
globular fruit
hopefuly ripening,
hopefully not killed off
by a frost.
Even now,
my leaves like toes
reach out
for warmth. Cold
nights and city
streets
have no glowing smudge pots
to leave traces
of soot
on the leaves and golden finally-ripe
oranges.
You are
the man with big hands,
the man whose brain
numbers every piece of hardware,
and who knows how to use any tool. A mechanic
you always come home dirty,
as if some flame had
been smudging you,
keeping your tender leaves from
low temperatures,
and I who grew up in a little house
frightened of soot and angry

at the voices of men in the night,
long for you
with all the mystery of my childhood.
You threw me out once
for a whole year,
and I felt that all the masculinity I knew about was gone:
       saw blades humming through stiff wood,
       the hand that threaded wire into place and made light,
       the soaking parts of motorcyles and cars which
       were sloshed free of old dirt and put meticulously back
       into now running
       machines,
       the hands and mind which could fix the shower
       or the furnace if either
       didn't work.
That year
I sought sunshine,
looked for men who could work in a foundry,
who were not afraid to touch hot metal.
And I was the orange
who began to love the dark groves at night,
the dewy shake of the leaves,
and who believed these burnings in the night
were part of a ritual
that might someday be understood.

And from the little girl who read fairy tales,
I have grown into the woman
in them, the one who steps magically out
of those fragrant orange peels,
into your house,
next to your side. I sort your dirty smudged work clothes
for the laundromat and long for the sun.
You are the voices in those dark nights, laughing on the front
       steps
into that clear fiery tequila;
and always there will be part of the child shivering in me

inside, knowing my mother feared something
that I must also fear,
her husband who left her alone for the salty ocean.
My father who walked away from me;
and then there is the part of me, that golden fruit growing on
the orange tree outside in the orchard,
searching for the warmth of the smudge pot,
and it is that part of me that takes your hand confidently
as we walk down the street and listens to your deep voice telling
stories.
Thank god for our visions.
That in our heads
we play many roles. There is part of me that trembles,
and part of me that reaches for warmth,
and part of me that breaks open
like mythic fruit,
the golden orange every prince will fight
to own.

1970

Sour Milk

You can't make it
turn sweet
again.
      Once
it was an innocent color
like the flowers of wild strawberries,
and its texture was simple
would pass through a clean cheese cloth,
its taste was fresh.
And now
with nothing more guilty than the passage of time
to chide it with,
the same substance
has turned sour and lumpy.

The sour milk
makes interesting & delicious doughs,
can be carried to a further state of bacterial action
to create new foods,
can in its own right
be considered complicated and more interesting in texture
to one who studies it closely,
like a map of all the world.

But
to most of us:
it is spoiled.
Sour.
We throw it out,
down the drain—not in the back yard—
careful not to spill any
because the smell is strong.
A good cook
would be shocked

with the waste.
But we do not live in a world of good cooks.

I am the milk.
Time passes.
You cannot make it
turn sweet
again.
I sit guiltily on the refrigerator shelf
trembling with hope for a cook
who dreams of waffles,
biscuits, dumplings
and other delicious breads
fearing the modern housewife
who will lift me off the shelf and with one deft twist
of a wrist . . .
you know the rest.

You are the milk.
When it is your turn
remember,
there is nothing more than the passage of time
we can chide you with.

c. 1971

Winter Ode

winter winter winter
there is winter in my heart
I am past 30 and winter is like my feet, frozen animals
in the snow winter winter
the name of everyone I love rings in these syllables
winter winter everyone I wait for is asleep
and winter is the winter of my aching throat
and my hands that look in the dark for something warm
to touch winter winter you remind me that winter
numbs me I cannot feel what I am touching

a friend a round a fat sun a man with red round face
blazing with ragged fire blazing with his need to be
the center of this system, he says
you hate young girls, Diane, forgetting that you yourself
are a young girl and I think of my wintery smile, my
eyes of winter that want to freeze all the young warm girls
of the world who are stealing you, the man I love, away from
me, those girls who take ancient husbands away from ancient
wives and the foolish ancient women they will become who will
lose their even more ancient husbands to other young girls
and no one sees winter, the deep winter, the winter of every
night alone of an empty house of gold snakes of chainy metal
that are warmer, more alive, touch me oftener than you, the
man I love, the man with winter in his ax, the man who puts
winter between himself and me the man who makes me ache with
cold, who makes me think of the moon, look at the frozen
    brook,
winter winter, a syllable of snow, a whisper in a blizzard

that is how my love for you is received,

like a whisper
in a blizzard.

I remember always the word
that defines my life
winter
winter
winter
winter
winter
winter

1969

Overweight Poem

biscuits with honey running down into the deep crevices
thick dark bread cut into fresh chunks and butter waving over the
    terrain,
red berries and yellow cream

am I thinking of these things
or you?

Love fills my body,
all the crevices
for the first time. And I feel
heavy
like the September limbs of an
apple tree.

Feel opulent

and don't like this opulence.

Coming from a man who knows less than I,
one who, like my father, talks big
and goes away;
one who, like my father, loves deep, a lot,
and goes away/has many others.
And I want it all.
A man who is everything.
Everything I can find in the refrigerator,
or the fruit bin, or the oven, or the larder, or the cup-
board, everything in the silverware chest, the freezing
    compartment;
I want him to be handsome and brilliant and
making a mark on the world, rich, responsible,
older. Someone to rescue me.

The British Museum, perhaps.

Something that will last well.
My favorite foods do not keep well;
must be gotten fresh each week.

I never know how far
for the sake of wisdom
to carry a metaphor.

c. 1965

Poet at the Carpenter's Bench

Building up
in any way,
a structure that will permit you to say
no,
a structure that will permit you to say
yes,
        as the thin small poet stood on the beach
        in the light of the torch and was
        run down and immediately killed
        that night, on the beach, the sand
        soft and cool, like his breath, just a few
        minutes before.

        Being around when somebody dies
        requires a leap of imagination,
        this reality too complete to comprehend,

        as when you left me

        and after that you were not in my life,
        though just the day before you had kissed me and touched
            my mouth
        with your large sculpturing fingers.
Building up
in any way
an organization that will permit you to say
no,
an organization that will permit you to say
yes,
        the poet who walked out on stage
        where there was a tattered American flag
        and a great man reciting the love lyrics
        of American poetry

        and he did it, just to throw that pail of rusty water

on the audience, a poet who walked backward
on the stage for attention
which he didn't get
and another returning a shaving kit of a shameless
lover with pimples/the broken glass was the least
she could include to indicate the hurt.
Building up
in any way
a structure that will permit you to say
no
a structure that will permit you to say
yes,
     as the poet who goes insane once a year
     calling for all his ancestors to kiss him on the mouth,
     because he has no imagination
     and needs their inspired breaths
     inspired into his mouth.
There are rituals
not structures
for being a poet,
       drinking too much, taking too many drugs,
       being a lady chaser, having your nervous breakdown,
       being irresponsible about money.
Structuring,
structuring and building,
building gradually and slowly
building a structure that looks like a building
     under the dim flickering candle the poet
     calculates the local sidereal time at birth,
     and makes a chart that shows moon—new and empty
     rising in a black black night,
     sun walking under the earth, naked,
     and all the other planets, not playing in pitch, no
        conductor
     for the orchestra, many players not in their seats
     when the performance is scheduled to begin.
You want to give him the benefit of the doubt;

you want to say he didn't deliberately ruin your life;
you want to say that he'll come back to you and love you in a
    black
lacy slip and put his soft mouth over your ear, the tongue
slipping in with words like love, sweetface, all the possessives
that keep you looking in his direction;
like a flower following the sun:
you want to think positive,
you want to wear your gold wedding ring
and wait for him forever: you're a damn fool,
you're too tight with yourself; you're a flower that will die
    tomorrow
dead lilacs sitting in the vase after a week, seeming to
smell a little like earth and the grave: poets, their images,
both men and women,
I, not less the poet, because I want to bury myself in the ground
and grow.

Building up
in any way,
a structure that will permit you to say
no,
a structure that will permit you to say
yes.
The poet is the passionate man
who lives quietly
knowing very well what he wants. It is love,
some formation thereof, a small rock
that he can carve all his life,
perhaps a house he can build with his own hands,
or one he can live in and shape around his body, as a crab will,
or a snail; he wants only one sense,
of love, of laying his eyes on the surface of the world
and seeing underneath, of love,
of all changes, all different roads leading to the same thing,
of love that never goes away
without coming back.

1966

The Duchess Potatoes

my people grew potatoes,
my hair is lanky and split edged and dishwater
blonde.
My teeth are strong but yellowish
I have little eyes
I am fleshy without muscles
my energy is thin and sharp like gravy
but I crawl into bed as if I were pulling a counter of rubies
over me,
dream past all my lower class barbed wire
walk down the street in a silk glove
try to scrub myself to an aristocratic bone,
and always come back to the faded colors,
lumpy shape;
you wonder why I refuse to type well like my mother,
or iron and mend clothes like my grandmother,
am offended by your boorish father
whose only virtue is that he's tended a machine faithfully
for 35 years and
supported
your beautiful mother
her strange children

he is a ghost of the peasant in me
of ugly linoleum floors
and a starchy diet. And I,
peasant,
have no compassion for the lumps,
the lumpy mashed potatoes
that weren't beaten with enough butter and milk.
and made so fine
so fine
they were called "Duchess"

c. 1965

164

Placing a $2 Bet for a Man Who Will Never Go to the Horse Races Any More

for my father

There is some beauty in sorrow
and the sorrowing,
perhaps not beauty
perhaps dignity
would be a better word
which communicates
life
beyond just what the body dictates
        food
        clothing
        shelter.
It is nothing that lasts.
It quickly turns into gloom, hate, resentment,
a burdening apathy
sometimes severity towards others;
but like a scarlet bird
from the tropics
suddenly seen flying in a New York City park,
so unexpected,
so unexplainable,
there,
different from its surroundings.

Caliente,
the poor man's race track,
in Tijuana, Mexico,
where I met my real father,
an old retired sailor
after 14 years of separation
and learned that the real pleasures of gambling
are knowing how
to lose.

Old man,
I place a bet for you
now that you're dead
and I am still living.
It is on a horse called "The Man I Love."
Gamblers are sentimental
so you will forgive me
living now
and giving away my love.
Win or lose
you played the races every day.
A certain spirit
I hope
you've passed on to me.

c. 1971

My Knees Go Before the Firing Squad at Dawn

Pain visits me
at night
like a workman going to his bar
for a beer
at five,
before he goes home.

It is
no extra-
ordinary event
is what I mean to say.

Pain comes in,
wearing his steel-toed shoes
and overalls,
and I try to remember
from his specific costume
what job it is
that he does
all day.
It is
not easy
for me to believe
in pain's necessity,
the aching of
my knees and back,
my wrists and ankles so brittle
I often fear they will chip
off and be gone,
like all the moving parts
the wheels, the arms,
of a rough child's toy.

Pain is a hard worker
in my house,

rising early in the mornings
and keeping track of every moment
of my time.

He is
perhaps
some ancient
head-of-the-household.
                         How I
wish I might take
him off
my income tax.

But no real benefits
accrue
except some foolish discipline
in my life. I have never
learned
to tell unwelcome visitors
they ought to
go away.

Never learned to tell
relatives
they are infections and diseases
to my blood.

You lower-middle-class hardhat
with narrow-minded opinions,
go away.
I can no longer afford
your wages
or inarticulate anger exploding
in my joints
and weakening my blood.
Pain
listens

like a deaf child
to my symphony.
Beethoven
is left
to only my ears,
aching
for some beauty.

1971

To an Autocrat

Today you told me
you kicked the first lady
you lived with
out
because she washed her underwear,
blue silky things,
and hung them in the bathroom to dry.

A few days ago
you told me
another girl got kicked out
for mentioning
grandchildren.

These anecdotes
about taboos
begin to extend from telephone calls
to toothbrushing
and leave me trembling
as I suppose you think a lady should
afraid to make any independent move.
There is no doubt
you possess this house
and everything in it.
You can move me out or in
at will;
have done so to prove your power.
My only weapon
is logic
which salts you like a withering garden snail.
                                        Because
it is you
who give me lectures
about the hang-ups of marriage,
and of people wanting to possess each other.

Save your stories for men,
I ought to tell you,
because any woman who buys them
is a guerrilla fighter who believes you've been master
of your house too long.
When you move all us silly ones
with our dripping underwear out
and install this one liberated lady with her fine panties
and spider-web bras,
her short icy slips,
and satin garters that draw your eyes up her legs
like filings following a magnet,
and you never see a vestige of how she launders them,
and she follows all your rules
and makes no demands,
while we poor offenders are always needing things
and trying to live our own lives too,
then,
sir,
I tremble for you
for real.
Will she cut your throat one night as you sleep
or take off your balls?
Will she steal you blind
and leave with your stockbroker
or debilitate you with your own weaknesses
and jump in to mastery after
she's spoiled you for anything but drink and talk?
She is your fate,
anyway,
if you don't realize
that living together
is what makes us human and decent.
We give in to others' needs, their rights,
making a fair division of privileges
and chores.
Our dog finds a long beam of sunshine

coming in an afternoon window
and she stretches her doberman body
to fit it.
        She follows the sunshine around the house
from morning to late afternoon,
stretching or curling into the patterns it makes
on the floor.
She is not perfect,
but she fits
the hours of the day.
                She understands
living/
        loving what you have,
making
the fit.

1970

Screw, a Technical Love Poem

"n. [ME, *screwe*; OFr. *escroue*, hole in which a screw turns < L. *scrofa*, sow, influenced by *scrobis*, vulva], 1. a mechanical device used for fastening things together, consisting of a naillike cylinder of metal grooved in an advancing spiral, and usually having a slotted head: it penetrates only being turned: *male* (or *external*) *screw*. 2. anything like such a device. 3. a hollow cylinder equipped with a spiral groove on its inner surface into which the male screw fits: *female* (or *internal*) *screw*."

Webster's New World Dictionary,
World Publishing Co., Cleveland, 1954

Sometimes I think of your father in his neat gangster shoes
sowing into your mother your eyes,
then the strange teeth touching blood on her ankles.
Turning yourself inside her
made you as graceful as a stillson wrench which can be twisted
into narrow mouths or
open ones. The joints of selenium, the moon's elbow
make you still
photograph me or any other woman who comes close / 34 I say is
the atomic number; when you find 34 women with 34
grams of selenium poured into 34
places — the knees, the fingers, the ear hole,
those delicate junctures of the pelvis.

Oh coming out of me is yards of piano wire,
unplayed songs. Dead keys unwinding.
My brains should have been wound around the machine screw
   with a square
head, or the machine screw with a round head or a
wood screw, or a lag screw, or a set screw but the hardware
cannot compete with the software
my brain, my throat, my anxious wrists / on the female side
I must wait for the proper motion it is internal
still impatience makes me want to push all the buttons,

flip all the switches, turn you on.
Yes, I technically want you and technically I can't have
you. How did life get so full of technicalities
when I only wanted to touch you but
found I didn't know enough formulas, did not have a low enough
atomic number, could not put out my hand
and say I love you because it is not a technical term.

c. 1970

On Barbara's Shore

for Barbara

The ocean has befriended me;
the rough white crests of waves walk
as if in moccasins
trailing a pale moist shoreline.
Knowing I cannot swim,
the ocean has not taunted me; instead
its rhythms and sounds fall like sea roses
at my feet. The singer
walks on the beach / the faces
who listen are cliffs of water. Tonight's concert
is over
but every day of life
is some concert
clear and beautiful.
Fish, like opal roses and the singed edges of tea-garden roses
and the camelia faces of blind roses, the roe of fish,
caviar and roses,
brush past me in this life. So confusing,
but beautiful.

When I wake up in your house
the serene white rug catches my eye. I know
it reappears from room to room
a thread of continuity in all your days and nights.
I dream of living in such a well-tended house
with Eastern rugs
tiles scrubbed to Dutch freshness
copper, brass & porcelain surfaces
sustaining the day,
but in such a life
the agonies of my past would be unexplainable.
And if life is to have any ultimate agony
perhaps that pain would be

the loss of explanation/of reason/of meaning.
The cockatoo sits in her brass cage crushing rocks against
her powerful bird's tongue.

There is music,
poetry,
dance,
in this house.
It is clean
organized
and direct in its meanings.
My life has none of this poetry to frame it.
And being in your house
eating your generous breakfasts
sleeping in your beautiful daughter's bedroom
and talking to you
makes me feel complete
in some way
as if
each of your movements were teaching me the beauty
of women.
I know you have some wisdom
dark as a frayed ancient book
setting off your fine face
which I have not yet learned. Perhaps your greatest beauty
is a form of hope
imparted to all who talk to you,
that life will yield its secrets
to the careful searcher.
Your movements are slow
and teach me
that they can be learned.
Music of the spheres: that means the planets moving in such
    harmony
that beautiful chords are heard in their concert.
Surely when you move
it sets up a similar music.

All life is motion.
Mine is the quicksilver flash.
Yours
some more steady beam.
The ocean
is my background. Its motion
designing the sand,
carving the rocks,
offering life to simple things.
Your house is an ocean.
A white bird curling its feathers like flower petals against its beak.
A sea which has befriended me,
even though I cannot swim.

1970

The Moon Explodes in Autumn as a Milkweed Pod

Is there a moment when the moon explodes in autumn
as a milkweed pod
wet wings of membrane unfolded
clinging to the polished seed,
sends light particles into the air
flying to some secret reunion
with the hidden parts of a man, woman
keeping her secrets
deep inside
a memory of you
explodes inside me,
your eyes when you wake up in the morning
having no guile,
beautiful in a way you are not,
leaving me always with the exquisite feelings
that you will touch me, the unequaled prince
from any fairy-tale
—your fingers more sensitive than any other,
but the artists's criterion is
what do you do with your sensitivity,
your perceptions

the door opens to reveal
an explosion under your pillow as you sleep
tonight, I tossing and turning
thousands of miles away
your eyes fastened to my picture, the lips
of which have been cut out,
this face,
is it yours or mine,
shatters across your drugged sleep
whatever name you take in another life
is pasted to a vial of medicine
but you cannot remember that I've invented
my life; you too forgot that once

and that's what all the trouble was about.
Where do you go when you want to get messages from me?
Don't answer your mail, your phones; I might
call when you are embracing another woman.
The task I set for you
was never completed; the plots we hatched
together never written;
there comes a moment when the moon explodes
as a milkweed pod,
the wings behind my eyes which are old
came wringing wet, rolled as a green leaf
slowing into existence
where were you when I flew away,
it was not a direction specified on a map;
I could not smile
at the old prognosticators,
like leaves of a calendar
showing that inevitability of days,

the secrets are there;
they do not show in the mirror;
underneath the circles in another man's eyes
is all the writing I need
to keep me reading law and poetry for the next
hundred years, but my rings
are less easily located, not confined to my fingers,
not in the form of circles under my
imaginary eyes; you know
where to find me,
always,
and I laugh to think I won't be there;
the secrets are
of course
how to get me there;
wings, wet, unfolded, cannot fly me,
the moon knowing the inside of my mouth as well
my name cannot talk back,

you too only communicate
from the sea of my sleep
I will not say you have left me alone; only that I
am alone
with myself.
It is always when you are
dreaming that
the explosion comes
scattering all the pieces of the map
into a new arrangement,
a new country.

c. 1970

Fanny's Cold Blue Eyes

I'd like to talk about you, Fanny, as a jewel
an object alone
with your glittering unreal gold hair
and your fake fur;
I'd like to talk about your blue eyes that are
brighter than everything else in a room
and only equaled by those of your son, my husband,
whose own blue eyes warn me there might be
some dangerous ocean, somewhere
as blue;
I'd like to mention your voice, Fanny, you singing
teacher without the courage for a career as a singer,
who tells me about
the offers for USO shows or Broadway musicals
when you weren't fat
and wanted to dance for an audience;
I'd like to talk about your voice, but I've never heard it,
only fantasies, plans for your voice, a voice
you might as well have choked in your throat for all
the good it's done you, your life, or
your family;
I'd like to talk about your glamorous flashing hands and
your pretty face but can only think of the daughter
with the beautiful hands and the son with the beautiful face
they made, and the vanity they passed on, and their
magnetism in the world—as they flash
the hands, as it smiles,
the blue-eyed face,
how they compel and people wish them good-will
and they never live up to their promises
except in images and smiles—
        where is the singing?
        where is the sculpting of new images?
        where are the words from the smiling face?
I'd like to talk about you, Fanny, as a bottle of rare wine,

but would have to say you were never uncorked
the light bouquet now heavy with sediment
and the metaphor is not suitable to your life,
because, though you should have existed as a jewel
alone,
glinting, reflecting beautiful light, giving off some even
of your own, I could not
say you have
or you do.
You married, Fanny.
You married, and your weakness kept you married;
to a slow, heavy, bad-tempered animal, Fanny;
and you're not any better, Fanny,
because your life has become just as slow and heavy
and bad-tempered.

Why didn't you become a singer, Fanny?
Because you wanted to keep your family together?
Or because you didn't want to have to work for a full living.
Oh, I know you work, you work hard;
but when you want to, and for what you want to;
have you ever had to work when you didn't want to
and at something you hated?

> I saw you panic with the idea that you teach full-time
> when I suggested that if you wanted to go to Europe
> and your husband might be out of work 6 months when
> you came back, that rather than save from his check
> you go to work full time for six months
>
> and yes I've heard the story from your daughter
> with the beautiful artistic hands she got from
> you about how you said once, when things were
> bad and she was an adolescent doing your dirty
> work, that you wouldn't be caught dead working
> to support a family

I remember that my mother worked full-time even when
we were babies. She hasn't your flair; she didn't
cast her burdens on her children.

Why did you stay married to a man
who beat you when the chicken wasn't cooked thoroughly?
who was jealous of your ease,
who tried to break you with demands, as he
felt broken by the world's demands,
who is so frightened and slow he received traffic tickets
for driving too slowly,
who was so weak he could only get a sense of power
by rabble-rousing and turning over cars of political opponents,
whom you could not share your life with?

And don't think that you are any different from him today.
Yes, I'd like to think of you as a jewel, Fanny,
but I'd have to think of you as a valuable diamond
which got hacked to bits with one fractional wrong-blow
of the chisel.

I look at your son every day,
a beautiful, strange man
with eyes like yours,
both coming from some exotic genetic ocean
and this is when I feel myself filling with anger,
feel it flowing out of me like lava,
because your ugly marriage
is that deformed fusing of you, Fanny, and your husband;
you could have left twenty years ago
and been a real jewel;
you could have sung your way through all the lights
but you didn't;
you could have been the star in a tiara or a necklace
and you're not even good for the chip in a wristwatch;
you could have worked and stayed thin,

rescued your son from his father, and most of all
what his father made you—it isn't beautiful,
it isn't a jewel;
it's fake hair,
fake fur,
a fat body,
a singer with no songs to sing, no audience;
a woman with no man,
and I fill myself with anger seeing it,
seeing myself with the same weaknesses,
the same passive peacefulness,
the same fantasies of a good life
letting myself help my husband, your son,
become more and more like his father,
letting him bully me rather than make his own achievements,
letting him rationalize his own inexperience with blame
and condemnation of my friends, my way of life,
my experiences, my talents

and I feel the anger bubble over and flow out every time I see you
thinking of how I will get old too,
fake hair,
fake fur,
a fat body,
a singer with no songs to sing anymore,
no audience,
and a woman with no man either
because a body, a bully,
a piece of sex, a bull
is no man.

I want to see you as a jewel, Fanny;
I want to examine your unique and perfect facets;
but it isn't the case.
I see only myself trapped inside a little glass box,
my own weakness keeping the door locked,
not making myself into a jewel;

an embryo, pickled in a bottle;
NOT being abused,
LETTING myself be abused.
There is nothing left for us, Fanny,
but contempt
and if we cannot feel it for ourselves
there is not even that ounce of dignity left in these bodies.

I'd like to talk about you, Fanny, as a jewel,
an object alone;
but the only precious stones left are your blue eyes,
your son's eyes now;
coming from a colder genetic ocean than
the arctic.
Cold, cold;
and I am hypersensitive to
cold.

c. 1968

A Winter Poem for Tony Weinburger Written on the Occasion of Feeling Very Happy

That Abomination in the By-Now 20th Century
Aesthetic Tradition:
Meditation on a Wet Snowy Afternoon

I have so much that I am supposed to do
that to sit down in this freshly-painted room,
listening to Beethoven, my own angry crazy father in time,
and dally around, writing about how happy I am
seems very laggard and un-American.
Besides, what is happiness anyway?
The snow was such a gentle covering on the ground last night
when we came home,
the beauty of city streets with their dirt covered momentarily . . .
but it is a beauty that is false
because it is gone so soon—

No,
that is the grossest of American sentiments.
Beauty is a moment of snow crystals
when no hand or foot has touched them
when they have not yet melted and carried grime and soot
into standing puddles.
Any instant is still reality.
Beauty. Who questions its moment?
Yet, I just said it was false because it would not last.

I could destroy our peace together
and the happiness I have just waking up next to you,
by thinking the American way.
And how can I write about such things as happiness & snow?
They seem trivial, foolish and sentimental.
Which probably means
they are
trivial,

foolish,
and sentimental.
But I feel safe here
exploring the maps of your imagination.
Love,
beauty,
both are the fulfillment of some deep longing,
a sense of completion
the hand
or the eye.
When I am alone
I realize that you are
for me
Beethoven,
Schubert,
Haydn,
and Bach, those sounds I cannot live without.
You are
that new snow covering our late-night street.
You are so different from me,
  a strong man who builds, thinks designs,
  a mechanic and architect,
  an important freeway in my life.
On this snowy afternoon,
I am happy to be in your house and feel
that it is mine too.

c. 1972

The Night Rides of My Neighbor, Lorca, That Prevent Sleep

Outside my window
coffeecups have scented the breath
that blows my curtains,
                sleeping,
                        leaving stained rings
                        on that counter,
                        my face.

Dreams move my countenance
as if it were earth
being pelted by rain.
With any horse he rides,
my dream must try to move as fast
and here I am
painfully awake
remembering
that I have been put in charge
of all the gold
in this world
              only I
can keep it polished
to its right
color.
Dregs of coffee threaten
to poison my lips,
to stiffen my fingers.
                  Why
have I been put in charge
of all
this beautiful soft metal,
this gold;
will I have to spend my days polishing,
or if not that, inspecting,
looking at cups,
handling rings,
waking up to find bracelets waiting at the foot

of my bed?
Have I
the strength to keep travelling,
have I the loud harsh voice to keep urging and scolding
those slaves, the mere owners of
all objects made of this soft metal;
it rustles in my sleep
like curtains. It clinks
like coffee spoons. It invades my knees,
ankles and wrists, threatening to stiffen me to the
breaking point; I dream
at night that the gold covers my eyes wetly
and seals them shut. Am I
the only one who can tell
when gold objects are polished to the right luster?
Am I the only one, Lorca,
that you can trust,
riding through the night, invisible, as you do,
knowing this world has forgotten blood on the lips
of your flowers, my own
soft lips bleed endlessly, darkening with clots
from all my angers, and yet my blood
is so thin, they will not transfuse it to strangers;
riding by
I hear you ready to stop again this night,
torturing my dreams with the restless steps I cannot
keep up with; you are coming to increase
my assignment,
to tell me I must be in charge of all the silver too,
for under my care the gold
of this world begins to
shine and remind us
of the desert and its simple ordering.
        Another dream comes to torture me.
        This time about rattlesnakes frozen and placed
        near the head of the bed; as I grow warm with sleep
        the snakes begin to thaw, their unstable blood to flow

189

and they will crawl down over my face.
Fighting with more hands than I should have,
I try to hold them off.
Lorca,
why are you riding around so fiercely,
frightening me
that the gold of this world
will tarnish and disappear
without my constant
articulate
care?

c. 1969

This poem is more properly a "dance poem" than a song or chant because the element of repetition is created by *movements* of language rather than duplicating words and sounds. However, it is in the spirit of ritual recitation that I wrote it/ a performance to drive away bad spirits perhaps.

The story behind the poem is this: a man and woman who have been living together for some time separate. Part of the pain of separation involves possessions which they had shared. They both angrily believe they should have what they want. She asks for some possession and he denies her the right to it. She replies that she gave him money for a possession which he has and therefore should have what she wants now. He replies that she has forgotten that for the number of years they lived together he never charged her rent and if he had she would now owe him $7,000.

She is appalled that he equates their history with a sum of money. She is even more furious to realize that this sum of money represents the entire rent on the apartment and implies that he should not have paid anything at all. She is furious. She kills him mentally. Once and for all she decides she is well rid of this man and that she shouldn't feel sad at their parting. She decides to prove to herself that she's glad he's gone from her life. With joy she will dance on all the bad memories of their life together.

Dancing on the Grave of a Son of a Bitch

for my motorcycle betrayer

God damn it,
at last I am going to dance on your grave,
old man;
       you've stepped on my shadow once too often,
you've been unfaithful to me with other women,
women so cheap and insipid it psychs me out to think I might
ever
be put
in the same category with them;
you've left me alone so often that I might as well have been
a homesteader in Alaska
these past years;

and you've left me, thrown me out of your life
often enough
that I might as well be a newspaper,
differently discarded each day.
Now you're gone for good
and I don't know why
but your leaving actually made me as miserable
as an earthworm with no
earth,
but now I've crawled out of the ground where you stomped me
and I gradually stand taller and taller each
day.
I have learned to sing new songs,
and as I sing,
I'm going to dance on your grave
because you are
      dead
      dead
      dead
under the earth with the rest of the shit,
I'm going to plant deadly nightshade
on your grassy mound
and make sure a hemlock tree starts growing there.
Henbane is too good for you,
but I'll let a bit grow there for good measure
because we want to dance,
we want to sing,
we want to throw this old man
to the wolves,
but they are too beautiful for him, singing in harmony
with each other.
                So some white wolves and I
will sing on your grave, old man
and dance for the joy of your death.
"Is this an angry statement?"
                "No, it is a statement of joy."
"Will the sun shine again?"

"Yes,
yes,
yes,"
          because I'm going to dance dance dance
Duncan's measure, and Pindar's tune,
Lorca's cadence, and Creeley's hum,
Stevens' sirens and Williams' little Morris dance,
oh, the poets will call the tune,
and I will dance, dance, dance
on your grave, grave, grave,
because you're a sonofabitch, a sonofabitch,
and you tried to do me in,
but you cant cant cant.
You were a liar in a way that only I know:
          You ride a broken motorcycle,
          You speak a dead language
          You are a bad plumber,
          And you write with an inkless pen.
You were mean to me,
and I've survived,
God damn you,
at last I am going to dance on your grave,
old man,
I'm going to learn every traditional dance,
every measure,
and dance dance dance on your grave
                              one step
for every time
you done me wrong.

1973

My Aunt Ella Meets the Buddha on His Birthday

She would like to roll down the aisles
of her church,
past the hard benches,
and in a frenzy
tell Sweet Jesus
she is holding his hand.
But though other members do,
Aunt Ella, in her soft
fried-egg body,
with two crooked fingers without nails
   (pushed into a machine in an aircraft factory during the war)
does not.

Her life,
       of course
cannot fit any testament.
Where did all the dirt come from
under the fingernails
when all she did
was try to lead a pure life.
     But a woman
     without a man
     is like a wild rose
     which blooms fast
     and flies away
     falls apart
     with the wind.
Her husband
killed in an accident
when she was like a new gardenia,
her skin white
the way girls do not like their skin to be today,
and her two daughters,
living despite her chocolate covered cherries
and true confession magazines

which warned
against all
that can happen in this world
where the innocent are butter
in a hot skillet.

      Helen,
           quiet,
                  with thick red lips and a pompadour
      married a sailor
      who ran off
      with his Australian mistress during the war.
I was a 10 year old kid
when Helen died.
The first dead person I ever knew/or saw.
The fact that none of us knew
how she died,
leads me to believe she killed herself,
the whispers were all there
but I wasn't old enough to piece them together.
Besides,
who ever tells children about death?
It is something we must learn about from
insinuation,
the innuendos of bitterness or regret
that make people say things
they don't want to.
Something must have happened
after that day her husband's plain plump mistress
came to the door and
said she was going to have a
baby
        this I heard whispered about
        in the pantry
        between my mother and Aunt Ella.
But they didn't whisper enough
after that

for me to hear
what happened to Helen
   or her thick lips
     that could have made her some Midwestern Protestant
      relation
       to Cleopatra.

Louise,
the other daughter,
married a truck driver,
6 feet tall,
who was often out of work,
who drank,
had other women,
spawned four children who all wet the bed
and had to come and live
with Aunt Ella.
Louise was a waitress
and she and her girl friend
died of carbon monoxide poisoning
sitting in front of the cafe where they worked,
in the old car,
having a cigarette on their break.

Aunt Ella lay alone at night
in the house with four grandchildren,
reading her true confession magazine,
praying and sure that those four
teen-agers were out doing
all the things
described in her magazine.
And I'm sure they were.
They lived a life that I,
scholarly, quiet, prissy,
could only be fascinated and put off by.

Aunt Ella had a friend, whom we called Uncle Noah.
He was a secondhand junk dealer,
a man who always wore a hat, something uncommon in Southern
    California.
My mother told me he was very rich,
but he never spent his money.
He had been trying for years to get Aunt Ella
to marry him; but she was afraid
he might take her to bed
and try some of those things
described in the true confession magazine.
They went to church together,
but never rolled down the aisles;
though they must have shouted to God
many times;
and called on Sweet Jesus
to have compassion and some mercy
on their souls.

The title of this poem is a lie.
My aunt Ella never met the Buddha.
On his birthday, or any other time. The Buddha
scarcely ever goes where she does,
and she
doesn't like foreigners.
It is actually a common trait
in our family; none of us
really likes
foreigners.
Now isn't that down-home
American?

c. 1969

197

Poem for a Little Boy on the Buddha's Birthday

You have
taken
a complete biography
in the form
of your mother's hand. Such a camera,
the lens
a blind measurer;
who cares
whether you will be president
if the coral scrapes
cuts the bottom of your feet as you walk
along the ocean floor,
who cares
where you are? Your mother never
forgets;
she does not however feel
the same salt.
             Is there anything
             more real
             than imagination?

She does not even
know where you are.

1968

Some Brilliant Sky

David was my brother
and killed himself
by the sea,
a dark night
without city lights
to obscure the milky way.

My hair glistens around me like stars
on the night when a man
cracks in half and falls
into the ocean.
Sheets of water,
as I come out of sleep,
no lover,
only the sweaty body of dreams

                    he stands over my bed
                    as I wake up
                    silent,
                    whispering to himself,
                    "no scars,
                    no scars,"

but he forgets
David who died in the ocean
when the stars were visible in some brilliant sky,
and does not see my belly
mangled with scars
from childhood or birth.

Poetry is our history.
We study the stars
to understand temperatures.
Life and death are the only issues;
we often forget that—
arranging our furniture,
washing our cars.

When I look at the sky
I think of David
throwing himself off that cliff
into an ocean which moves with the moon,
dying,
the red blood in his mouth
in a night as black
as eels.

1972

In the Secret Room, East of the Sun, West of the Moon

I met a magician
there,
measuring waves of light,
reflecting mirrors against my wrist
and touching me in the dark
of my own night.
I asked him for formulas,
remedies for my invisibility,
offered to trade him
the cap of darkness
for the magic ring
which would lead me through a garden
where flowers had daggers concealed in their petals,
the birds were flaming objects hurled against
intruders in the night,
and where a dragon named Love
guarded the gates against anyone
who had ever shed tears.
                              But he
would not trade,
saying,
it was not in his power.
And he sent me away to an island
where the sun only shone
one night of the year,
where there were no moons,
and the only light was phosphorescent, glowing
seaworms
which crawled up on the land
looking for something
nameless and beautiful
at a signal from a dragon named Truth.

But there were no magicians here,
or astronomers.

They were all somewhere else,
playing tennis with their glamorous friends.
I ate marigolds
and went home,
no longer afraid of anything.
But sad.
Feeling the loneliness
of my cold name.
I live in a secret place,
behind a carved door.
My house is a diamond and my life
is unspoken.
There is music that rescues us all,
and light into which
we all fade.
Life is its own metaphor. Silence speaks
for itself.

1972

When You Throw Amber into the Well of the Moon

A face looks out at me
from the water,
a lion shaking his mane and roaring
with anger at his watery trap.
And I reach my hand
into the water,
       like the slender trunk of a palm in the
       distance.
In the water
everything disappears.
Like a child in a crowd.
But the moon is death.
Its cold rocks fill my belly as if I had
swallowed songs of birds
and awakened in a tree.

When the sun died
it still lasted for thousands
of our years.
Magicians study it now,
while poets fly off to the moon.
My lion is trapped
in the water
which is desire.
And I throw my hand in
to rescue him.
But my hand cannot play tennis
or golf
or even the piano, anymore,
it is a useless hand
to a lion.

The crab sitting at the bottom of the well
looks up at the lion,
his eyes on stalks that are longer than my arms can reach.

He
is in his element.
Does not understand our struggles.
Music and poetry
only reach the ears
of those in anguish.
The silent crab
needs nothing
but the boom of the surf,
the pounding of waves,
even in the quiet well.

1972

Driving Gloves

for Anne Winters

I wish my past had been
a volcano,
       spewing me out on a shower of hot sparks,
but it wasn't.
I came from a sad family.
I tried to run away,
and I thought I made the probable
improbable.
But that was a fancy,
a short-lived sweet-pea, climbing up my back fence,
like a girl's summer organdy dress,
worn only once or twice.

Some of their sadness
had to be in me.
Throw these lines away.
Vines that did not flower.

A bud is not a summary.

But it is the total
in a reduced form.

The perverse mimic/ the desire to repeat
whatever's heard
or seen.
The genes,
some big sound studio,
a memory eye,
a stain from Mendelssohn traced through the fluted pea
family.

I learned to drive a car when I was thirty-two years old. I went back to California where everyone but me was driving by sixteen, and, twice that age, I hired a teacher, hired a car, and learned to drive. It made me feel free. I hate clichés, but when you leave your life alone, there is nothing it can become, but a cliché. From the beginning, I insisted on what my friends considered an affectation. I wore gloves for driving. I said the wheel got too hot or cold, that my hands got sweaty or stiff from rheumatism, that I did not feel in control without gloves.

In California, almost no one wears gloves or a hat. They are considered affectations. Especially in the lower classes from which I come. Yet, I remembered this December, while driving to California from the East Coast, after four long years of being a licensed driver, that my mother, improbable as it seems, used to wear gloves to drive in.

My mother, who went to a one-room school, who lived in a house with a dirt floor, who never wore gloves on any occasion I can remember, who never wore a hat, who never had any place fancy to go, who never even had a job she had to dress up for, she, she wore gloves when she drove a car.

It is the perverse voice that speaks in us,
going back to old inflections,
old fictional
language of other characters . . .

Your father, Anne,
has written what?
                    ten
unpublished novels?

Surely,
a noble action
we should all admire?
That a man could continue doing for himself
what most of us only do
if the world approves . . .

And he
is a
terrible driver, you say/
disapproved of by all the family?
They shudder when he hits the road,
or did you say,
he doesn't have a license any more?

And you're like him
you say?

That's why you are over thirty and letting me assist
in winning your driver's license?

And you reiterate
how we're all like some parent
or ancestor

But your father also
had four wives,
or was it five?

And you have one husband
a faithful one you would never leave.

And didn't you say your father taught English all his life
to students who had a hard time reading
and writing
and you,
you're a Greek scholar,
a speaker of three languages,
a "bluestocking"
                if we use that term any more.
And your only associates are people like me,
all of us finding the illiterate
a painful chore.

Yet,
what are these mimicries that we all look for,
that we fear?

The one thing that has terrified me in the dark
every night of my life
is the thought that I would be like mother,
she, who only read the *Reader's Digest*,
that I would look like her
        heavy and unfashionable,
that I would talk like her
        in a high polite voice
        and worse,
        have nothing interesting to say,
that I would be condemned to a life like hers,
        a sad life,
        discreet of imagination.
But here I am,
unaccountably,
with my driving gloves.

Some stain Mendelssohn found,
like the mole on my left shoulder which has its mysterious twin
somewhere.

You don't want to drive badly, Anne,
or write unpublishable books
or spend your life teaching
the unteachable.

I don't want to spend my life like my mother,
    unable to get along with people, yet convinced that I
    need them,
    working all my life at jobs I hate and which do not pay
    much either,
    insisting that I love everything, anyway,
    claiming to love my children
    parading my sacrifices
    for them.

Talk, talk, talk.
Do we have no courage to live our own lives?
Do we hope the past will live them for us?

No, Anne,
you learned to drive because you are not your father.
And why do I wear these driving gloves?
    because my hands are arthritic?
    because I want to feel like a professional driver?
    because it is a safety measure?
    because my mother did?
No, I wear them, Anne,
because I like to wear them.

Our lives *are* our own.
We must assert it.
We must ask grace from ourselves.
Our memories.

Let them
release us from the past.
What is the past, Anne?

Only something
we have all lived
                    through.

c. 1973

Cobra Lilies in the Supermarket

for Wallace Stevens

I wonder
as I am driving to the Market Basket
why I have lived my life
as I have.

The mother of
my third husband
            —a blond blue-eyed singer, she was—
told me
I was a crybaby
because,
at the time,
I was crying.
She said
you should fix up your life
and then not cry
about it.

My own mother
said, referring to my fourth husband
                who left me
"What are you crying for?
Buy your own house so that the next one who leaves you
won't be able to take your home away."
And she too said,
"You always were
a crybaby."

When I cry now
it is usually in anger. But
sometimes
I still cry in pain. Then I hide myself in rooms where no one
can see me.

I bought a house
but cannot live in it.
My fifth husband says he would leave me
before living there,
and since he is a nice man
(or perhaps it is just that I am older)
I didn't cry,
nor have I recently been called
a crybaby.

I still live in other people's houses,
listen to their music,
live out of suitcases.
Driving to the supermarket in the rain today,
shopping for someone else's dinner,
I wondered if anyone ever felt
he had a home
other than in his head.

I was tantalized with the cobra lily sitting next to the oranges
& avocados like a purple clenched fist
unrolling its tongue
but unwilling to speak to me, I thought.

When I studied the piano
I always cried at my music lessons.
My teacher stopped criticizing me.
I heard that secretly she called me
a crybaby.
I gave up piano,
took up voice instead.
Now, my lessons are concerts
where crying is considered an art.
I shout,
I speak,
I whisper,
and at last again

I can cry.
This time
no one taunts me
but other crybabies;
and when I am alone
I defend myself with poetry:
"I remember the cry of the peacocks."

1973

The Story of Richard Maxfield

He jumped out of a window.
Or did he shoot himself?
Was there a gun,
or was it pills?
Did anyone see blood?
Was he holding water in his lungs?
Or was he right about the CIA conspiracy and killed by one
of them
because he knew their plan?

Richard was an electronic composer.
He wrote a piece called "Cough Music" made up of the coughs
of hundreds of people at concerts.
He was brilliant and well organized.
And then he fell apart.
He was homosexual and took drugs.
He was brilliant and well organized.
I loved "Cough Music" and could not see how such a fine
composer could fall apart as Richard fell apart.

That is the story of Richard Maxfield.
He died in California.
It did not make me as sad that he died
as that he fell apart.
We all die.
We do not all fall apart.
"Cough Music" was a beautiful piece of music.

I went to a
concert tonight
and heard many people coughing,
especially during the encore which was a piano piece by
Debussy, delicate and sparse,
like a dress you can see through,

214

and everyone seemed to have to cough
during this piece.

If you cough very hard,
do you think you fall apart?
I once had a bad cough
and now realize that for two weeks I coughed during every
poetry reading and concert I went to.
I wonder if anyone recorded my cough?
I wonder how many readers and performers
not only did not feel sympathetic towards
my bad lungs and the symptomatic cough
but also wanted to shoot me for coughing?
A fortuneteller once said I would die of TB. I wonder if that's
why I like "Cough Music"?
                                    Perhaps I should have my lawyer
write into my will,
                    "I would like to have 'Cough Music' played
                    at my funeral."

Someone would think that in bad taste.
No one likes to think that after you die you still have
bad taste.
Even if you had it in life.

What bothered me the most about Richard Maxfield was that
he had the bad taste to fall apart;
dying after you fall apart is actually a rectification
of bad taste.
Richard was so brilliant and well organized
I could not imagine how he fell apart.
And "Cough Music" is just one of his very beautiful concrete
tapes.
They say the men he loved destroyed him.
But he was brilliant and well organized and I find it hard
to believe some not-brilliant and poorly organized man could
destroy him.

You see, the story of Richard Maxfield is one I do not
understand.
But I have always loved "Cough Music"
and when I heard the beautiful Debussy tonight
and thought of a man I love
who for many reasons I cannot see or be with
and I heard the audience coughing, flashing every once in a while
like light catching a strip of aluminum which blows on a fruit
tree,

I understood that I would never fall apart,
though I did not know why,
and for a moment I thought of the involutary action of
coughing, and I understood perhaps
why he jumped out of a window,
and I also refrained from coughing, though just at the end of the
Debussy,
          I wanted to/   maybe just to join the whole crowd.

There are many ways to die,
but none of them is subtle.
                    Why *do* people cough so much
at concerts?

I cannot touch the piano.
I cannot touch you.
If the King of Spain gave a concert
no one would cough.
The story of Richard Maxfield is one I do not understand,
but I thought of it tonight,
listening to people cough their way through Debussy.

It was not music.

Only Richard Maxfield made music out of coughing, and he is
dead.
Richard Maxfield is dead.

1972

216

Virtuoso Literature for Two and Four Hands

Nothing is simple or innocent any more
except poetry and music.

I.

Memory relies on emotion.
No other part of the mind does.

A night near New Year's Eve, in New York City.
I do not remember if it was raining,
but it was either cold or damp,
weather that affects you like someone tracking mud
onto your freshly scrubbed kitchen floor,

and my life was falling apart,
that is
the man I loved was running away from me
as if I were a
leaking ceiling or a broken step, and he,
a homeowner, fatigued,
eschewing one more repair.

A party in a prosperous uptown apartment
was something to do,
voices, faces, fragrant and effulgent,
like gardenias on a hothouse tree,
forced in a December greenhouse,
the story of that night is a story of waiting,
a story of waiting for a hand which was not there
to touch me on the shoulder and say, "Let's
go home," a story of waiting
for a carpenter in a land where there are no
trees, a story of waiting,
waiting,

except for one moment which I remember,
like an afterimage from bright light:
a man,
an old friend,
a writer and teacher,
sat down at the piano/ he was drunk and nostalgic,
and bending over the keys like the limbs of a willow,
he played "Stella by Starlight,"
here in this company of intellectuals and poets,
he forgot where he was.
He forgot the rain and the evening of talk,
and played as if he were in some 1940s piano bar,
a song none of us knew the words to,
here in this company of intellectuals and poets
he played "Stella by Starlight"
this man who read Blake and Reich and Vallejo,
who listened to Bruckner in his spare time,
who did not believe in popular art,
even Bob Dylan or the Rolling Stones whom we all listened to.
He sat there
and with reverence
played "Stella by Starlight"
And I remember that part of the evening better than anything
    else.
Though I later went to a jazz club and heard exciting Pharaoh
    Sanders,
though I later sat desperately with a man who asked me
why,
why I was faithful to that man I loved,
the one who wanted nothing to do with me,
and I could not answer.
I could not answer.

II.

I could not answer,
because the simple answer,

the true answer,
was one I could not believe.

                    Nothing is simple or innocent any
                    more, except poetry and music.

A night near Thanksgiving,
in Wisconsin, snow crystals blowing through the air,
an owl in the nearby woods
reminding me that I am alone,
"a woman alone"
(my mother always referred to herself as "a woman alone"/
I learned it was a desperate and terrible condition).
I visit friends.
They too have a piano in their living room,
gleaming in the dark, like brandied cherries
in a flat french bottle.

Whenever my life falls apart, I am reminded
that I still have not fallen apart.
The owl, speaking alone in the woods, the one
we never see; we know he is waiting for a small soft creature
like a mouse, to snap the backbone in half,

                        and that this
is not cruel but simply his means of sustaining life.

The piano glows in Mary and Walter's living room,
the luster of the wood is like well polished boots
promising the hands and feet someplace to go.
I feel the energy of the piano and remember my old friend,
writer and teacher,
who sat down and played,
so lovingly,
"Stella by Starlight"

          sun
          moon
          stars
          minerals and fire which liberate us from
          earth & water

and I tell them my meager story,
wondering why we are not satisfied with our minds
unless our hands can do their share.

As if in a story, myself,
I tell them of my promise when I was twenty-one
not to touch the piano again,
to take the motion of my hands
and transform it
into the energy of my life,
and then I confess that I feel the piano vibrating in the next
room, like a nova, an exploding star, one whose heat and light
I cannot resist,
and I go in to the piano with my hands on fire
and sit down and play old Chopin preludes/ my fingers have
not touched the keyboard for fifteen years,
they do not respond automatically,
but they remember patterns, they remember rhythms,
they remember chords and keys,
and they do not wait,
they do not wait,
they touch the keyboard, I sway, bending my body like a willow
tree, one which will weep for me.
I do not know "Stella by Starlight" but I know Chopin,
and I let my friends hear me,
how badly I play now
I remember the pleasure of touching

                    sun

                    moon

                    stars

                    that owl lonely in the woods

                    obsidian and ivory

                    the hard rocks of life

they did not ask me
why
I do not play, why I am faithful to my promise
though touching the keys means so much

to me.
They knew I could not answer,
or rather,
that I could
but that my answer
would not be an
answer.

III.

Nothing is simple or innocent any more,
including poetry and music?
                  My friend, the astronomer, cannot rec-
                  ognize the constellations in the sky.
                  They are not math or science.
                  He honors truth,
                  not poetry.
A night in spring,
Colorado mountain air, like razors near the cheek,
my husband and I entering a mountain resort bar,
a place where they serve beer in half-yards, steak and kidney
    pie
is on the menu,
              the entertainment is an old lady
named "Juneau Hattie" who plays ragtime piano.
We sit among business men and college boys,
someone from Sigma Chi having a birthday,
middle-aged tourists drunk and revealing marital fears,
      "My mother was afraid I would marry the first man in
      uniform who came along . . .
                  and I did."
drinking Irish coffee,
            thin and steamy against the cold night
outside.
We are together and happy.
My hands move along with the piano player's hands.
She is thumping out

"My Wild Irish Rose," "Take Me Out to the Ball Game,"
the exposed hammers above her keyboard moving
the way they must move every night for her.

She is over fifty, wears a green silk dress, Hong Kong style, slit
up the sides; and a little green hat she may have made herself.
Thin legs, like sticks, under a chunky body. Spindly arms
that hammer out tunes we members of the bourgeoisie can sing
together.
I think of her playing every night, every night having
to be gay, a party, wondering how she can do it,
knowing that we all
always
are on stage,
that we all do it,
though each day gets harder.

How can she bear to play those same songs every night,
put the same emotion into them?
My friend and I,
the man who played "Stella by Starlight," and I, who was moved
to confess to the keys my longing for them last winter,
could we be moved
more than once?
He,
had he played "Stella by Starlight" any time in the past ten
years?
Will he again,
in ten more?
I,
holding my hands away from the pianos I have passed,
like a hiker in the hot dry mountains refusing to open his can-
    teen of water until he is absolutely sure he could not continue
    without it,
taking a sip,
and saving the rest for another
desperate time,

222

I yielding that one night to Chopin in winter
and knowing that I would not be so tempted again
for at least fifteen more years . . .

Drinking Irish coffee, listening to this music-hall performer
who probably makes little more money than will pay her rent,
buy her Irish whiskey;
                    sitting with a man I love,
one who cares for me,
wondering how
we renew
our emotions each day,
wondering what it means to have a simple desire
with a simple response.
                    Nothing is simple or innocent any
                    more, except poetry and music.
When I speak,
I hear many other voices,
like a tv store with the sets all tuned to
different channels,
When I listen,
I no longer can identify voices,
often
do not know the words of songs,
cannot remember
the names of
pieces.
When I type the word "piano"
my fingers often slip.
They spell "pain." Oh,
how do we do it?
                    Get from day to day,
when nothing is simple or innocent,
not even poetry or music?

c. 1974

223

Tango-ing

As If the Ballet Russe Would Ever
Have Looked at My Square Body and
Funny Feet

This man
is tall and slim
and confesses   that at twelve
                                    dancing school
he could do   all   the steps.
If he had been born wealthy
and lived in the '30s
he might have spent every evening in a tuxedo,
dancing in nightclubs
                    the Flamingo
with a reputation like Nero Wolfe's secretary and sleuth,
                                        Archie Goodwin
for being the best dancer on the floor.

I,
I have dreamed for years of dancing *Swan Lake,*
for years have mentally lifted my legs and pointed my toes
next to a wooden bar, the mirror a great deceiver
to anyone with imagination,
and it is with chagrin
I look at myself here in real life,
a chunky short peasant with magical square feet
and a fear of my body
which makes me move awkwardly.
For years,
I have dreamed of my other self,
told stories to make her real.
You, apparently too,
like an imaginary life
tango-ing across the dance floor
                        Coconut Grove

The Starlight Roof of the
Waldorf Astoria

Funny,
for I see you
tall,
slim,
the man who could do those things if he wanted,
whereas you can only see my body
as it is.

Funny,
too,
that you should love me
in spite of my incredible squareness;
and I, you,
for the imaginary which in my mind
is already achieved.

I think of all the dancers I have known,
one leaped out of a window   to his death,
all have lost husbands or wives,
one dances in agony for a set of mutilated, dying intestines,
one showgirl   now drinks rather than dance for no admirers.
What can I say?
That I loved trying to learn to tango with you last night
alone in our dark quiet house,
with me humming the tune & beat?
And that I was glad to sit down laughing at my own clumsiness
ten minutes later,
knowing you did not love me less,
for one more act
I imagined
yet could not perform.

1974

Blessing Ode for a Man with Fishbones Around His Neck

for H.M.

Armillaria mellea,
honey mushroom,
let it grow by your door
and be edible

Pileated woodpeckers,
tall and handsome,
may they return in abundance
and nest in your hollow tree

Mercury,
the liquid metal,
let your mind follow all of
its forms

May the cow vetch move aside
when you walk in tangled grass

May all the women of the world
show you the shining white insides
of their slender wrists

May the buildings of the world
each be built with a special
room for you

May the shoes of the world
never bind your feet

May your name be spoken
in the places where good mechanics dwell,
be they poets or motormen or carpenters,

for in that company, fame is
a judgment to be proud of

May you never breathe the air
of a place without inspiring
some of the language of its animals,
the forms of its trees and flowers

May your maps continue to be read
by all serious travellers

This blessing be said
by running water,
near a beam of sunlight,
in the presence of the lady's daytime moon.

c. 1974

Walking Past Paul Blackburn's Apt. on 7th St.

I wanted to take a walk
and think of the city
whose only remaining beauty
is that you wrote about it.

I bought an ounce
of Carpathian mushrooms from the mountains
of the Ukraine
in the store beneath your old
apartment
        Paul, for you,
        these gestures:

I walked into the store,
seeing in the window a string/ many strings
of powdery white mushroom caps,
brown-gilled underneath, among the amber
and big crocks of honey, nestled next
to embroidered ribbons of purple green red
yellow and blue, simple
puffed blouses and thick books with gold letters.

"How much for a string of mushrooms?" I
innocently asked.

Wonder. Awe.
          "A string?" A pause.
  "We sell them by the ounce,
and they are light as a feather. But a string —
$30 maybe?"

"I'd like an ounce then," and he put them in
a tiny paper bag which might have also held a
child's glove
or a marshmallow.

He smiled and told me how delicious they were;
how they would swell up and fill a soup,
how choice they were—only the caps

Paul, I walked out
thinking how you have taught all of us
to dwell in this city and
to make friends with our neighborhoods.

Hello, Paul, I hope you have
found the ultimate
city.
Or maybe you have wisely moved to the country
in your old age?

1974

Preface

DEAR MICHAEL,

Like Egypt and the Sphinx, you have been part of my fantasy life for the past two years. I suppose all that means — and I do not really know why I should tell you or anyone this, since the beauty of our fantasy lives is that no one can take them away, they being totally private, and even poets have fantasies they do not share with anyone . . .

    all that means is that I must have met you at a time and in a place when I needed an image, an idea to cling to, in order to live with some difficult reality, and that you must have had the right mustache or voice, read the right poem, or touched me in some special way.

The most real connections I have in my life right now, and perhaps that is an ideal, are by letter. I think I'm looking for something different from anything I ever wanted before, and letters have become more real than any of the people I know. I have discovered too, that all poems are letters, and

nothing is simple or innocent anymore. Except poetry.

MEMORIES: FANTASIES

    lovers
    do not love,
            tho I suppose travellers travel
            and losers lose.
I am only a traveller because there are places I need to go;
and when I met Michael
I loved another man
whom it was impossible to love.
He rode his motorcycle
on a dirt track I called
Allegory.
It was in my living room,

and my own name was Moon,
One Who Finishes Far Behind In The Race,
but I owe him everything,
even the memory of the ocean full of cascading fish,
their silver bones like keys in my pocket,
their shining skins gleaming on my arms as I rode
through the night
behind Motorcycle Rider,
with a helmet of broken promises, dripping down on my
    shoulder
as trout and smelt and wiggling sardines.

When I met Michael,
he was a surprise,
like finding a silver snake in your bed and not being
quite sure if you did like snakes;
he was a mustache
and a pair of shoulders,
an image
like the moon
            to remember on a dark night.
                        Do you remember Michael?
                        I said to a nameless hiker
                        on another dirt track?
                            Yes, he kissed
                  you.

No, I say,
you are thinking of someone else;
a motorcyclist who lives in the New England woods.

Ramble.
I ramble on this dirt track. Not called Allegory
anymore
since I am trying to remember Michael,
a man I made up in my head,
my brother,

who jumped off a cliff into a California ocean,
too young for a mustache, memories, or
poetry.

Lovers do not love.
Or they find that love is something to fear,
something to run away from,
a snake under a bare foot,
a silver trap which catches a moment of light from the moon,
just as the paw of the mountain lion
passes near it;

if lovers do not love,
perhaps the losers
do not lose
either.
Is there any way to lose,
when there is certainly no way to possess?

In my mind,
I own you
hoard you,
save you up,
do not let anyone know
what amount of you
I have.
Do not let anyone know
that what they think I have lost
is really only the head of the sardine; I have
in my mind
memories
of a whole,
            leaping,
                  shining like a keyring,
                              silver as a thumbtack,
uninvented
fish.

Telling You True, About My Fantasy Life

for M.W.

Wdnt let anybody
really know
what I think when I turn out the lights
at bedtime.

Or sit in airports
waiting
for planes.
        How I turn you into the
racing car driver
who will pick me up at the other airport when my plane
lands,
    or see you
as the man with the black mustache
and heavy tweed coat
walking up the ramp, American or United,
with an expensive camera
and a copy of *The Wall Street Journal*;
who smiles at me
when I drop my copy of *Road and Track,*

or how I close my eyes and pretend that I am lying on a beach
with a gorgeous tan that makes the scars
which show above my yellow bikini
gleam
    and look exotic
rather than ugly,
and that you are with me and we are making love,
tho never in my life have I been on a beach
where it was private enough
to make love
        yes,
        that's fantasy for you,

it would be boring,
no doubt,
for you to know that
I have often pretended some man I was with
was you
            so that I could talk more
engagingly,
so that I could be interested in him at all;
or if he were so hopeless that I could not imagine
his ever being you,
then I would pretend that you were standing on the
other side
of the room,
watching me as I talked to him,
until my face became animated and the things I said
were like dreams or poems
and you, the unseen audience, with your cynical smile
and diffident manner,
would let me know you were watching,
tho you'd never say anything,
and I would walk past you, on the way out of the room,
going I suppose with the boring fellow to dinner,
or to sit in a bar,
and smile at you and wonder what you thot, as you nodded,
diffidently,
again,
      ironically,
            actually,
                  and then I would realize
that even the imaginary you
which I invented
who was not even standing there
had also disappeared,
as I walked out of the room,
and that now I missed my own invention,
as much as I originally missed you,
                              the source

of my invention.
Oh, and you would never believe
the physique I invented for you, though I can scarcely remember
if you are tall or short,
broad-shouldered or thin,
and the fact that when I dream of fucking
you are often the man doing it,
though I have never met a man, any King of Spain, who liked
to fuck as much as I do
                    all women, according to a good poet I know
                    are nymphomaniacs
                    when they get a chance
but since I live with you only in my
imagination, I am privileged to invent you as someone
meeting my specifications.
My imaginary scenes with you are always arrivals and departures.

The man I love
must simultaneously show his love for me
and be cool about it,
but the part I always get best, in my fantasies
is the being cool part,
and even in my imagination, you often walk away
with some other girl,
or alone,
or have not been wanting to touch me
as I wanted to be touched.

This explanation is addressed to:
          The King of Spain
          My Motorcycle Betrayer
          The Woodsman
          The Astronomer
          A Poet
          A Truck Driver
          A Mountain Climber
    and you,

who have no name,
and fit the silhouette of all the above,
putting your arms around me when I am cold,
so that I smell the tobacco smoke in your clothes
and feel assured that a man might take care of me,

                             someday.

My body is ugly.
My face, not beautiful.
My conversation topical and limited.
Sometimes I try to believe in my imagination,
but when I reveal it,
the poor rag reads like *Esquire* or *Playboy*
or worse,
The Ladies' Home Journal.
And yet I still believe in the tree which made the pulp
for all this poor paper.
Don't pity me.
I am proud proud proud.
And honest.
Honest,
like a dormant volcano
you've trusted
too long.

1972

Precisely, Not Violets

for the King of Spain

I only mark
the lonely ones, days when time slows down
and reminds me
of an ageing face.
I remember a girl with a bunch of wet violets
from a past
I do not know I lived.
And in this rain,
there is one footprint that does not blur;
the King of Spain,
following me,
invisible, of course,
yet not making me cry,
as you have,
M, the man who has left,
taking only the spider plant
and a french coffee pot, an antique table,
a marble ball,
an old inkstand,
and your clothes which used to fill many hangers.

Books, yes,
you took many books, but my house is full
of books. Books are my life. Grow in the corners
of my rugs and walls,
like violets in the spring.

I, too, am a book,
and you took the expensive hand-bound copy of that with you
to bury perhaps, under a stack of
fashionable volumes of new poetry.
But my house is still full of books,
in manuscript and folio,

bound and unbound,
and I, the original book always there
with too many publishers.

The word.
I live by the word.
You gave your word,
and now
have taken it back. Is that like a book going out of print?
Because no one will buy it?
If I could curse myself to silence
I would.
But without my tongue
violets would grow on the floor of my mouth and only
make you leave me
for different reasons.

And what have I lost
in losing you?
Not the King of Spain,
for he follows me everywhere.
A book, perhaps.
An idea.
The illusion that I could ever be loved,
as I have loved.
Or that love is any more
than a rabbit the hunting cats have mangled and left
on your back porch?

I only mark
the lonely ones, days writing out of a silence
someone not named Beethoven
put in my head.
Violets grow around my lips. Wet with
spring rain.

Their blue reminds me
of the beauty
solitary things
can have.

1975

Fifteen Poems for a Lunar Eclipse None of Us Saw

I. Not the Blood a Dreamer Kissed from My Mouth

Wanting to make music
as if each note could be cut into shape;
as if an arm manipulated a shoulder and hand
and objects could come as clean
as ideas.

Wishing beauty were not owned.

Wanting a rose to be
more original.

And the moon not so old that it was
decaying tomato-red, soft mush
when my fingers clean out the vegetable
bin/ the moon I put in there
firm, round; not the blood a dreamer kissed from my mouth.

II. The Dream

A dream / like a fire truck
with a dalmatian sitting
by the chief

      two men love me
      more than their own lives

      the arrow
      which was shot into my
      heart

      blood in my mouth
      thick as porridge

      and yet I did not feel
      as if I were dying

      one kisses the blood away
      from my mouth / his own
      face retains a smear
      what does the other one
      do? For I sense both of them
      as loving me.
      Yet only one holds me,
      cradles me, kisses
      the blood from my mouth.
      The other
      is only present

      I feel I am loved by two.
      Yet only one
      does the touching.

III. WATER

yr element,
the ocean, a metallic plate
on which all the bread
in loaves as big
as whales
is cut.

      Scorpion's tail,
wet earth,
and desert sand

            cactus in the foot
like stars
sitting in the palms/
No diamonds fall
from fingers or toes.
Only your smile reminds me
it is water I love
and the shining creatures
which live in it

      sting ray
      manta
      dragon fish
      coral devils

even their housing
yielding
to water, that big
soft pressure.

IV. WRITE

a letter
once in a while," he said.
But words
would not come.
Black lines on paper
were symbols

      moons burnt out at the end of a hot night
      sun flowers with charred faces
      stars like old teeth
      which fell out of a rosy mouth

when words are more important than food,
being
the only reality,
the only tangible possibility
for survival,
they become the diamond dogs
rising and running
out from the ashes.

My letters would be terrible
in their insistence,
coming more often
than meteor showers,
                but filling
the sky.
Obscuring the steady planets
and old constellations.
New suns, new galaxies,
but nothing that could be called
coming
     "once in a while."

V. For Michael, Armoured with Roses

Roses covered Lorca's breast.
Roses blossomed on my lover's hands.
Roses were in my own mouth instead of words.
All the blood drawn from history's thorns
could not transfuse life
where life does not want to be.
It is the fragrance,
the textures, I love most.
Only blind men need color. But, of course,
you know I am going blind.
                                    History.

VI. The Lady Who Sang

Her name was written somewhere in cobwebs.
Her songs were written by spiders.
Sometimes the moon applauded
but mostly the moon slept
simple and quiet as porcelain.
She drank roses
and held thorns to protect the man she loved.
Michael rescued her
with a rope of pearls thrown down into the well
where she was drowning.
Lorca kissed her lips.
Someone threw emeralds over her feet
as she lay.
Her songs were filled with the snails
which climbed up the old well walls, and carp,
ancient fish, the small frogs
which shared their voices at night.

She is invisible
but Michael sees her.
The lady who sang
sings a song for only one man.

VII. THE DARK CLACK OF MORAYS

*"A three foot Moray Eel, from the
coastal waters of Lower California.
Large specimens can inflict dangerous
wounds with their strong jaws set with
needle-sharp teeth."*
— World Book Encyclopedia

The dark clack of morays like dead leaves on the ground.

The dark clack of morays like dead leaves on the ground.

VIII. LIGHT

The roses glowed in the room, and she wrote by rose light. Her eyes were candles. Her fingers had diamonds in them for none to see. Roses bloom in every place like snails in a rainy season. Listen to me: light from roses is not unusual. Turn out all false lights.

IX. Sun with Hands for Rays

You big sun
touching me like you own me
I will put rings on all
your fingers
weigh you down with
jasper and malachite.
You big sun
my lips are bloodstone
sardonyx.

And just wait till you see all the
bracelets.

X. DONNA

Mary called them buttonflowers. I called them by the name of stalky, worrywort, broadstraw. One name is never enough for me, for I learned young that names are everything. Thus, many names are many treasures.

One name:
a fortune,
or death.
Call me Diane,
moon,
silver archer,
huntress,
pillar of marble.

XI. THE ROSES WERE TALKING

This time she was able to hear them
though she had been deaf all these years.
Her fingers were crystals.
The roses were talking.
But all they said was,
"Breaking, breaking,"
and some would have sworn it was the wind,
or just imagination.

I found that I wanted nothing
from people,
but their lives;
for poetry,
music,
even the roses
are the antithesis of labor.
When work is play
then it might become art.
The flowers will never tell you this.

XII. Eat Your Rose Hips, c'est la vie

Once there was a spirit
who took the form of a poem.
However,
since poems in the 20th century
often seem formless,
this caused a great deal of trouble
for the spirit.

XIII. POETRY, THE UNPREDICTABLE

You ask me questions
that I can answer.
They do not satisfy me,
like the packages of seeds sitting on my desk:
Anaheim sweet peppers and mammoth dill from Ferry-Morse
     Company,
seeds I may not even plant, and which surely have
very little chance of growing well for one who travels,
plants in pots, and then has to leave
the pots for others to tend.

My green thumb excites me
for there is no answer to why some things grow and others don't
and botany classes never really taught me why some plants have
     buds and
others don't.

I only know that roses excite me
and other growing things.
And the ocean at my door, behind my windows,
in these fingers;
that is a sound.
I love it / yet it frightens me at night.

The unknown,
the mysterious,
those of us who need to know
everything,
find that
the more we know,
the more things we don't know
excite us.

Poetry?
Surely the most unpredictable?

Like the roses
of our landlord's
which did not get eaten
by worms.

XIV. DAVID

There is a swirling scribble
in my desk's blotter
which looks like a fingerprint
from some large hand.

I know its source
(a pen which would not write,
my hand's firm pressure engraving
the spiral lines into the soft green face)
yet looking
just now
I thought perhaps
it was you, David,
who had returned.
My brother,
dead all these years.

XV. Western Music

I don't want to be
a fool about this: but the moon seemed to be floating
on the ocean this morning,
early
before I awoke,
before I walked down to see
that watery surface
I could not survive in.

Why do I remember this,
living in a rain forest, where snails and slugs
try to invade the bathroom,
where the shower is growing pale green orchids,
and where Michael's hand often
has mushrooms
sprouting on the knuckles?

Surely salt
kills moon creatures.
The pillar
a mirage
in the desert. Rain
only a rhyme
from a french form,
the tonic chord
in this Western music.

1975

The Skier

for M.B.

Squinting eyes
against the hilly snow,
you are red-gold and thin enough in
the hips to bend like the tail of a lizard,
the cold winter full sun
lighting you up in my mind.

You stand,
battered and beat up
from a day on the slopes
in your down parka
at the end of a bar, full of faces like camomile flowers in a bare
    field,
drinking bourbon.

Girls eye you,
as if you are the last piece of devil's food cake,
knowing your body is hard and fresh from the snow,
tingling in the knees and hips,
flakes frosting your eyelashes.
They watch the slope of your shoulders,
as you turn away from the bar,
thinking of the winter hills.
They know you are ready
to take one of them to bed and
to move all over their own bodies, as
white slopes,
small hills, powdered mountains,
sliding icily,
           flushed burning with the heat
of dry ice.

I, non-
athlete,
non-skier or swimmer,
warm singer of icy chants,
I watch you
and talk with you
and, when I dare —
                    touch you,
knowing,
for an instant,
about this cool sport;

but I was born with inner-ear upsets,
have only an odd grace
that stumbles
with no real sense of balance.
Skiing would exhilarate me for one minute
and surely kill me
the next.
I have none. No sense
of balance.
I could scream with pleasure
in that first rush down a simple white hill
and then in an instant
hit a tree or twist my bones,
breaking hips that are already brittle,
cracking my back or neck like a chicken,
those parts of me which always give dull pain
in any weather.

Yes, I liked hearing
about you,
and surely desired you
more than you could ever have wanted me.
But I am smart enough to know
I am no skier,
that you could not love a stumbler

257

on the slopes,
that I could not ever give myself
wholly to
any sport,
                save perhaps one . . .

Hello there,
beautiful skier,
I am here alone,
in a dark house,
watching snow fall over winter hawthorne and elm,
thinking of this wintery world,
— how
        I like looking out of
the windows at it,
thinking,
not touching,
knowing the pain of too many
cold failures.

Loving you,
thin, red-gold,
with all your other girls,
for your natural,
deadly,
athletic,
American
wintery
success.

1975

George Washington's Camp Cups

*"Be kind to yourself," she said
last February. "Don't forget
the small things. The good
book. The cup of tea."*

And that winter at Valley Forge
was one
we must all weep to remember.
Shoes ragged,
coats growing thin.
The food diminishing. Meal full of rot
and worms.

General Washington, my father,
for his comfort,
had sixteen silver dollars cast into cups,
small cylinders for drinking
grog,
sailor's drink,
soldier's fuel.
And I suppose some would sneer, with revolutionary zeal,
at his looking to his own comfort
when men were starving,
freezing.
        ("Eat yr vegetables, dear,
        Think of the starving children in
        India.")

The same ones who sneered at me in the '60s.
        ("How can you write poetry
        when the world is falling apart?")

As if,
somehow,
this were the first time

the world had been
falling apart,
and there were something I could do
to mend that great tearing.

Surely not,
tho?
Or how could we be here, spinning
with silver bombers,
and heavy lead feet out walking on the moon's powdery surface?
In this age of technology,
I wonder that
Humpty Dumpty was so impossible to put back together
again,
for tho he would have been ragged and scarred,
and not the old innocent egg,
surely, there are means of rescuing,
recycling?

Change?
Growth?
Have we ruled them out of the world? Must
only the smooth,
the brand new
be viable?

"Be kind to yourself.
Don't forget the small things.
The good book.
The cup of tea."
But oh, the pain of that admonition,
reminding of the difference between an adventurous vacationer
exploring exotic Elba,
and that broken crumpled toy soldier who was exiled
there.

I have drunk thousands of cups of tea
this year.
And from George Washington's camp cup,
lots of grog.
The mid-West hears me reading books
while, like a siren, my voice floats over the waves at Laguna
    Beach.
No ideas of order,
but thoughts of love, of losing it,
                              of the pain.
George's men were starving,
freezing,
in a fight most were too young to understand.
He, writing his letters every morning at 4 a.m.,
his warm grog steaming out of the silver dollar cup.

Outside a winter window,
the King of Spain,
not properly dressed for a blizzard,
in his gold shoes, thin silks and frozen mustache,
still leaves his footprints.

"Be kind to yourself," I admonish everyone,
waiting for my cup of tea.
And I wait for the King of Spain,
dreaming of George, my father,
of Beethoven who rescued me,
of David who is dead and buried on a California beach,
and of all the beautiful men I have loved;
for loving is
the secret; not
being loved.

What virtue in the egg's new smoothness,
except the beauty of perfection in birth;
I want to see Humpty Dumpty put back together again,
to love him for his ragged, jagged edges,

and the yoke scrambled with white.
Evidence of living.
Evidence of life.

George, I toast you.
M, I love you.
Beethoven, I want to hear you at Key West.
Be kind
to yourself,
all of you.
Don't forget the small things.
The good book.
The cup of tea.
An egg, put back together again, not
by magic,
but by patience, effort.
Love.

1975

Those Mythical Silver Pears

for Steve

I remember a past
of playing Beethoven sonatas
in a dark house over the water,
and lights from the hills surrounding me
instead of the arms of the man I love.

You remember playing
basketball,
tall, Egyptian, silent,
a stone figure,
no one ever talked to.

Neither of us
ever lived outside our own heads,
you trying to do what you thought others expected,
I trying to coax love out of the keyboard,
you throwing baskets
where there was no hoop,
I imagining a music no one could hear.

We sit together in your kitchen
which is dark,
not full of the life of someone who cooks,
a photograph kitchen,
I drinking
with my feet up on the chairs, the way I like
to sit, and thinking of the girls
next door, in the other lighted kitchen,
the ones who must think you are handsome, who idealize
tall men,
who have gone to basketball games and cheered,
though they never saw you there then.

This is the painful story of two imaginary people,
living like lions in their heads,
but the world sees them as Sphinx,
silent,
locked into mineral,
surrounded by desert and night.

Women fantasize a life of love that cannot exist.
Men, the competition of games and seduction of crowds.
We set up a world no one can question:
the past,
our private diaries.

If we were sitting in your kitchen eating, right now,
you would be drinking a glass of
mercury.
And I, biting
into one of those mythical silver pears.

1975

Ode to a Lebanese Crock of Olives

for Walter's Aunt Libby's
diligence in making olives

As some women love jewels
and drape themselves with ropes of pearls, stud their ears
with diamonds, band themselves with heavy gold,
have emeralds on their fingers or
opals on white bosoms,
I live with the still life
of grapes whose skins frost over with the sugar forming inside,
hard apples, and delicate pears;
cheeses,
from the sharp fontina, to icy bleu,
the aromatic chevres, boursault, boursin, a litany of
thick bread, dark wines,
pasta with garlic,
soups full of potato and onion;
and butter and cream,
like the skins of beautiful women, are on my sideboard.

These words are to say thank you
to
Walter's Aunt Libby
for her wonderful olives;
oily green knobs in lemon
that I add to the feast when they get here from Lebanon
(where men are fighting, as her sisters have been fighting
for years, over whose house the company stays in)
and whose recipes for kibbee or dolmas or houmas
are passed along.

I often wonder,
had I been born beautiful,
a Venus on the California seashore,
if I'd have learned to eat and drink so well?

For, with hummingbirds outside my kitchen window to remind of
    small elegance,
and mourning doves in the pines & cedar, speaking with grace,
and the beautiful bodies
of lean blond surfers,
dancing on terraces,
surely had I a beautiful face or elegant body,
surely I would not have found such pleasure
in food?
I often wonder why a poem to me
is so much more like a piece of bread and butter
than like a sapphire?
But with mockers flying in and out of orange groves,
and brown pelicans dipping into the Pacific,
looking at camelias and fuchsia,
an abundance of rose, and the brilliant purple ice plant
which lined the cliffs to the beach,
life was a "Still Life" for me.
And a feast.
I wish I'd known then
the paintings of Rubens or David,
where beauty was not only
thin, tan, California girls,
but included all abundance.

As some women love jewels,
I love the jewels of life.
And were you,
the man I love,
to cover me (naked) with diamonds,
I would accept them too.

Beauty is everywhere,
in contrasts and unities.
But to you, I could not offer the thin tan fashionable body
of a California beach girl.
Instead, I could give the richness of burgundy,

dark brown gravies,
gleaming onions,
the gold of lemons,
and some of Walter's Aunt Libby's wonderful olives from Lebanon

Thank you, Aunt Libby,
from a failed beach girl,
out of the West.

1975

To the Thin and Elegant Woman Who Resides
Inside of Alix Nelson

Curly-head,
plump little mother's girl,
like a delicious peach in August,
and now yr pit wants to burst out
into a Vogue model with peacock eyes and slinky hips that
are like swan-necks, even in the bulky clothes from Autumn Saks,
this is an invocation to dump
fashion,
to love your own soft peachy cheeks,
to show your white arms like sweet pillows
and to let men be lovers,
not faggots.

      (Oh, yes, Thom Gunn, who protested that word in
the *New York Review of Books,*
I *will* use it.)
For now is the time to proclaim

                     men AND

women
as lovers; and to proclaim
our own Rich
American bodies,
filled with healthy vegetables,
and marbled Charolais meat,
the rich red wines of France,
and the stinging white ones from California.

Now is the time to love flesh, for once a country has produced
flesh that it does not deny or destroy,
civilization has come a long way, baby.
Every sophomore writes poetry. And every truckdriver watches
    Bertolucci.
Every housewife plays the harpsichord,
and most businessmen know philosophy and chess. So,

can we live with these punishing ideas,
that a woman with a boy's body is beautiful, till she has to starve
herself on rye-thins and non-fat cottage cheese. How can my
   husband
with his Pancho Villa mustaches and divorce papers in briefcase
put bells on his pants and work out at Vic Tanney's while taking
   off
his wedding ring, trying,
like all of you,
to be slim.

A critic of life sent me a letter this week, denouncing my thin
   lips,
and the life of constant movement. But I am like water
or fire,
never still. Yet, she has never
seen me.
My sturdy Polish, German, American body, filled with sausage
and cheese and wine, always sharp from the vinegar of salads and
   pickles
and spicy from the hot food I also love. Love is
substantial.
Love, I say,
is sturdy and lasts longer than anything else.
She complains of my thin veneer,
but I am a new painting,
not an old one.

Allow me my American prerogatives, I say.
Forget faggots and their thin bodies.
The confusion of Pentimento.
Clarity: like Goethe,
I want more light, more clarity, more vision.
And I think of my California landscape,
the thin palm trees on their pencil-like stalks, which are imports.
The fat stubby palms, which are native to the landscape.

And I will not diet on toast and lettuce, for my lettuce is
leafy and fresh, from endive to chicory, with cilantro and cress,
and tossed with crumbled roquefort, thick fresh olive oil from
the Mediterranean and vinegar aromatic with tarragon.
My body is full of the juice of poetry.
I am not even thin from lack of love, for perhaps what I have
learned is that Americans,
we, have so much, we all love too much,
or, perhaps, better stated, not "too much" but more than anyone
can ever receive. The generous givers.

Alix, inside your body of pears and peaches, and mine of a thick
leafy salad, is delicacy, yes. But never thinness.
Let us picket Weight Watchers.
And throw aside Fashion. Give us the rich chorus
of American drama. The substantial narrative, the loud Country-
Western singer, not the thin lyrics of an English past.
We took clotted cream and spread it over our bread. Butter,
meat, vegetables, too.
I will not starve myself
in order to dance on European yachts, for we have our
square dances here. And hoe downs. And most of all,
the dance of our daily bread.

Give us this day . . .
yes, and forgive us,
as we forgive those who want us to be thin. For this is the
kingdom.
Yes, and the power and glory
forever.

Ah, men.

(The sigh of a well-fed woman).

c. 1975

Some Constantly Besieged Castle

Note: the lines "Next time we meet, / let's keep our clothes on" are from a poem presented in one of my poetry workshops by a New York poetry student named Binnie Klein. I was so tantalized by the lines that I assigned everyone in the workshop to try to make a poem out of them. I felt they were a good example of useful lines buried in a bad poem. Alas, I was the only one to do anything further with them, but am grateful to the workshop for giving me the opportunity to make this poem.

Next time we meet,
let's keep our clothes on.
Let's not touch,
letting our bodies be like seashells
empty of soft mollusk life,
or even a hint that it's a possibility.
Let's not even spend the night
in the same city,
for surely I would come tiptoeing to your door
in the middle of it,
in spite of my good intentions,
like water seeping under the sill,
a quiet flood breaking over your large
sailor's body, as the
phosphorescent wake behind a slim boat.

Let's not be in a room alone:
we might fall silent as a deserted barrier reef
and turn into coral hunters.
Scratching hands and legs in an attempt to break off
pieces of our own simple body stone.

Let us surround ourselves with others,
so that we can talk passionately
about the subject of love,
showering sparkling drops around the room,
without soaking each other,

                                    as groupers,
big sea bass, travel the seas,
with many smaller fish swimming along
for the nourishment.

Next time we meet,
let's both be married to other people
and not in danger of being on rafts alone
in the Atlantic.
Because your naked body
excites me as if
I saw a vision of a Spanish galleon,
with full sails,
moving towards me during my morning bath.
To touch you, is to find a worn creased map
that promises Ferdinand's ruby chest.
To feel your presence,
is to change all conversation,
as our words are changed under water.
Next time we meet,
let's keep our clothes on,
as nakedness symbolizes a kind of terrible innocence,
and my feelings for you have no innocence.
They are ancient, heavy, sexual, historic,
as a 100-year-old carp,
swimming in the moat
of some constantly besieged castle.

c. 1974

Recognizing That My Wrists Always Have Salmon Leaping for Spring in Them

for Jason

"Betrayal?"
            he asked me/ the
one word ending
in a question mark.
What *do*
I mean by that?
Surely not
simply
that someone could not do what I expected of him?
As,
there are no strings attached to love,
no rights or reasons to expect others to feel
as you do.
            It was a cold February,
            wet, snowy streets,
            fire burning in the fireplace & cognac
            spilling across our throats,
            my mind was a dogsled to the arctic,
            my wrists had salmon leaping for spring in them,
            I could always return
            to fire & ice,
            but would the barking dogs drown out
            the splashes in my pulse?

No,
no,
betrayal is not so simple—
a breach of faith,
an abandonment of loyalty,
a promise broken,
implying that

273

first
the promise had been made.

And I aching for the mechanic,
the man who rides motorcycles through the dusty craters
of the moon,
        races with the sun,
                wearing salmon bones around his neck,
who left me for trees he will cut down,
& a pond which seeped away last spring,
thinking of my hands
against the body & face of the arctic
which is my life
the fire
in that stone fireplace burning —
    what?
images of myself as false expector.

I tried to talk of betrayal
but could only think
of how impossible
yet necessary it is
for us to expect ANYTHING
from other human beings.
The question
pulled my mind very fast,
the runners of the dogsled skidding
over years of snow.
In my wrists
the salmon return every spring
and lay their shining eggs.
We are faithful always
to ourselves,
those leapings and slidings which take us
somewhere
we feel
we must go.

1973

274

On the Subject of Roses

California shakes its petals/ poppies
are lying against the hills,
orange in their careless motion,
like goldfish swimming in and out
of an aquarium castle.

Bad music
gives a bad life. But no one
should have to choose between Mozart and Beethoven.
Yes,
a brilliant day is
necessarily
one with flowers.

No, Mozart
and Beethoven
were not rivals.

c. 1977

Reminded of One of Those Girls I Never Was

Each night
I work late
washing dishes
or cooking for the next day
tidying floors
or closets
waiting for your midnight knock.
I go to bed finally,
alone,
under my yellow blanket.

Like the sun,
it shatters my wrists
and brushes my ankles.

The King of Spain
comes climbing through
the nasturtiums
in my window box.
Or perhaps I simply know
he is near
the pungent smell of the orange & yellow squashy
flowers.

He is not you,
of course.
His gold tooth making him distinct
from any of my other
lovers.

Perhaps you will never
again
knock on my midnight door.
The beautiful blond boys
I moon and yearn for

knock once
then return to their
bronzy girls.

This afternoon,
in the bar,
I saw the slim hand of a pretty girl
slip around your calf
as you stood next to her table.
And I too
wanted to touch
your serious tall legs.
But the nasturtiums growing in between
the narrow joints of my knees flashed
their yellow orange bitter ripe odor
then,

I felt covered with flowers.
I laughed,
talked loudly,
looked for my invisible
jealous lover,
the King of Spain to come walking
in the door.
I frightened myself with my own
compulsive talk,
wanting,
wanting,
wanting,
you.
Seeing that other hand move
around your calf
in such a gesture of familiarity.

Each night,
I work late,
reading,

sometimes writing,
waiting for your midnight knock.
But when it does not come
I turn off the lights.
My nasturtiums shrug their
waving silver dollar shoulders
and the squashy yellow-orange
flowers send out
their salad fragrance
into my night.

I have,
thank god,
I have
my faithful lover,
his gold tooth flashing like flowers.
The King of Spain.
And he loves me,
as you do not.
As no man ever has.
He is always there,
waiting, faithful,
more beautiful than the most beautiful blond boys in their linen
    sails.
The King of Spain
whom I met once on a California beach
when one dark man
was pulling a nail from his foot
and another was racing on a track with starfish.

Each night
I work late
waiting for your midnight knock.
And though I know you will never come,
I do not turn off the lights or
open my door,
even to the King of Spain,

until I know
it is too late,
and you are home sleeping
with one of those young
beautiful,
bronzy
girls,
one of those girls
who reminds me
of what
I never was.

1976

Standing at the Door

At the door,
we are saying good-by.
To the old, the young look very soft.
Like rabbits,
or deer,
the soft pets of children.
Thus, in your grey track suit,
though you are as tall as an oversized refrigerator, I see you
in the way we view
small, soft things.
Yet, we embrace a little like a small woman and a refrigerator,
two bodies made of such different materials,
each equally unyielding. Inappropriate.
Not matched.

An incredible silence in my life
has left me with this image.
One I keep turning over and over in my head.
Of the embrace which means nothing to you and which, to me,
is another sign of failure.
You have not shaken my hand, at least.
A gesture I have been horrified by
since a lover departed, shaking my hand, not saying
another word.
Yet, we are not lovers.
And should not be. Why do I think of you,
my student,
in your grey track suit,
tall, blond, from the same little town in Southern California
    where I grew up,
a young and very nice man,
who understands kindness perhaps better than any man I've ever
    known,
or at least is willing to show it truly,
as few men are?

And I, perhaps as shocked by kindness as by a lover
shaking my hand,
freeze
that moment in which I wanted you as a lover more than
    anything in the world.
Freeze it,
with my stiff body,
like one of the bodies in all of those murder mysteries I read,
leaning away from you,
afraid to touch your kindness.

In retrospect, I have to realize
how false the linking of sex with violence is
for most women.
For my body was alive with sexual feelings,
feelings that if I touched you,
I would melt into you,
like some foolish description out of *True Romance,*
and so I held back.
That moment frozen. Me, holding back,
stiff,
rigid,
a small person,
from your tall body in its grey track suit, and I know now
what I felt was love
for your kindness,
for that gentle concern you had really shown,
even the kindness
of being curious about the identity of the man who shook hands.

We did share a sexual drama.
And I was not the teacher then,
or you my student.
You taught me that men can be kind,
loving,
and gentle. And you did not desert me
when you left me,

though I have not seen you since.
Your gesture was one of loving, not leaving.
Making up, finally, for
the man who shook hands.
Teaching me my own responses are true.
Reciprocity a puzzle for us all.

I think of you,
tall as a refrigerator,
and wonder if I unconsciously think of you as cold;
know that my interpretation is wrong.
You, a preserver, like the best Frigidaire,
and I,
you allow me to continue with faith in this world where chilling
    preserves
prevents spoilage and waste,
where it gives continuity,
my favorite Meursault chilled for its best fragrance,
and the low temperatures my most beautiful plants
thrive in.

c. 1976-77

Overnight Projects with Wood

for all the plumbers, carpenters, & mechanics

Lined up
like chocolates in their perfect paper jackets,
the boys on one side of the room.
The girls,
little shelled filberts,
on the other.
The girls are going
to home economics for the first time.
And the boys,
to shop. To manual training.

But you thought "manual training" meant learning
to be a man.
And thus today you are a carpenter,
plumber,
mechanic,
woodsman.

I,
I knew that home economics
had nothing to do with being
a woman.

Now two friends speak to me.
Rilke, with his jet-black mustache curling like a scythe,
smiled this week as he told me he won a silver dollar in sixth
    grade
for building the best birdhouse.
His father, the tailor, had just built a house in Ohio,
and the wood, like scraps from a new suit,
fresh and unscarred, made a house
snug beyond the dreams of a poet.
When I see him,

he jingles the lonely silver dollar in his pocket,
a medal for his beautiful hands.
And he feels no need to build a house of his own.

The man from Receiving, at Sears,
did not begin his birdhouse until seventh grade.
And though his book promised this as an overnight project
this birdhouse required two years to become a
chaotic tower of babel.
Or, so he says.

I have all these stories from men,
while I remember my own perfect blanket stitch, and neat
  patching.
A good batch of biscuits.
Tho I rebelled against making a nice apron, cut a hole in the
  middle of it,
and mine was, thus, too disgraceful to be shown on parents'
  night.

Oh, we were all little ice-cream sundaes then;
butterfingers,
or creamy fudge.
Such babies,
such children,
thinking, dreaming.
You, of manhood,
Rilke and his brother, the man in Receiving at Sears,
training for wisdom.
I,
what was I doing?
Making my own perfect blanket stitch,
patching neatly,
making good biscuits,
And rebelling, rebelling, against a plain apron.

1977

Life Is Like a Game of Cards, Or
Another One of Those Metaphysical Statements from a Distant Reader

for Al Greenberg & Wendy Parish

I said to Alvin,
"I like to play games, even tho I never win.
I somehow feel that they reflect life,
and one thing poetry has taught me
how to do is embrace success when it comes,
while not getting too upset about failure."

He agreed with me.
Of course, secretly, he thought I would be
one of those people who won a lot but just
downplayed it.
Was he ever surprised when we played
three games of Oh Hell or Oh Pshaw, as it is sometimes called,
and he won all three. And, in fact,
I not only lost but came
nowhere near to winning.
But I enjoyed the games.
Drank a lot of cognac.
Ate popcorn.
Thought about how many things I was a failure at,
including love and marriage,
maybe even life.
How everyone is disappointed when they meet me,
because I really am ugly,
and I really am plain,
and I really am
fairly dull,
just as I've said
(to great rhetorical effect).
And every day I live with the knowledge
I've disappointed someone
who expected something better from me.

It's not true that people don't want to play cards with you
if you always win.
That actually challenges them.
What embarrasses them,
what they dread,
is to play with someone, like me,
who always loses,
usually good-naturedly,
hiding whatever chagrin I feel
somewhat successfully.

I call up Alvin and ask if he and Wendy
want to play cards again this Saturday.
"No," they say,
they have lots of work to do.
I sit at home and read.
I've always known the truth
about everything.
But I carry on.

Pain. Yes, isn't it a burden to get
from day to day?
But how to respect anyone
who willingly gives up that struggle?
Anne, Sylvia, John, Virginia,
you were cowards. I'll say it now,
and get it over with.
We all suffer.
It angers me to hear only those cowards who give up
spoken of as "sensitive."
How much more dignity, power,
we must have to carry on, precisely when it is
too painful.

When I was young, I also used to like to play games.
But my little sister, who was younger and perhaps not as smart,
always ruined the game by quitting

when she was losing.
It angered me so much once I tried to beat her to death.
Now I never see my sister. I still try to find people to play games
    with,
and I never quit when I am losing.
Tho others so often seem to refuse to play,
as if they fear I will always win.
Alvin,
I don't understand the world.

I sit alone
in a garden of wild California poppies,
their simple silk leaves against a brown hillside,
waiting, waiting,
for the King of Spain,
knowing that fantasy lifts us all
beyond pain.

1975

The Pumpkin Pie, Or Reassurances Are Always False, Though We Love Them, Only Physics Counts

Pumpkin,
freshly scraped out of its tightly adhering
orange skin,
as if you tried to scrape
beach foam off the sand,
the seeds washed and set out for the birds on the porch,
churned in the blender, after baking to watery
pulp in the oven.
                  Fresh
pumpkin
in other words,
not that bright yellow stuff
that comes in tins,
and ready to make pie.

Enter this cook:
the experienced artist who grew up
with tin cans and a cupboard with only two
spices—salt and cinnamon.
It is my first time to make a pumpkin pie
from pumpkin.
The tin can being so much cheaper,
the time required, so much less.

How do I say this:
    cooking smells,
    as the flakey crust is baked,
    and I am stirring the custard filling,
        pumpkin pulp,
        cinnamon (my spice),
        nutmeg,
        ginger,
        allspice,
        cloves,

the delicious thick cream,
sugar,
eggs,
oh good things, and I am
stirring, stirring, not allowing
any lumps,
the spices wafting out into the house and
feeling the perfume of the kitchen,
thinking that men make better cooks than women
because they have ideas about what they do,
not feeling the simple urge to fill up or provide
a meal,
stirring, stirring, thinking,
wondering what the man I love is doing,
thinking of different kinds of skills, thinking
also
of a poet who writes about music and water to-
    gether,
stirring and wondering,
wondering
why this custard does not get thick,
and finally the correct amount of time being passed
and the custard seeming thicker but not as thick
as I think it should be and knowing that
when custard starts to get thick
it gets thick really fast,
right away,
so hastily, with Mercury whizzing around my heels,
pour it into the pie shell,
then think with horror, what?
if it doesn't
get thick?
And it is an hour from dinner,
lots of guests,
and not enough cream to do the whole thing again.

I wait.
Women know about waiting.
Artists know about waiting.
Lovers are the only ones who never learn
about waiting.
But even they often
have to wait.
"Please tell love to wait for me,"
says one of the great poets,
but love never waits for anybody, at least
not in the rain,
oh tears,
oh metaphors.

Anyway,
I wait.
Test the pie filling with a knife.
Not a silver one,
because this house has no silver,
I have never had silver,
but test it,
no good.
It still isn't firm.
I put it in the refrigerator.

I wait.
I take it out after anxiously waiting,
which means I didn't wait very long.
Oh, this perfect gourmet's delight,
something even the pilgrims seemed to be able to whip up,
and I in this modern house
worrying and wondering,
has poetry really informed my life?

I have not been waiting long enough.

Anxiously, I say to a lady who has been hovering around
the kitchen,
            "do you think it will set?"
She looks at me reassuringly,
as you would look at a child who wants to know
if daylight will come again,
a lady whose husband has said that pumpkin pie
is his favorite.
            (Did his mother use pumpkin out of the can?)
I now think I should have strained my
homemade pumpkin pulp through a jelly bag to get out
excess water
            oh techniques,
how they do us in

Reassuringly, my catechism is answered:
            will the pumpkin set?
            of course
            do you think it will be okay by dinner?
            of course. it will be delicious.

Of course.
Dinner. A menu I will not describe. Delicious.
Preceded by many drinks, many
appetizers, accompanied by much wine,
much laughter and flirtation,
a party occasion.

Dessert.
Pie out of the refrigerator.
Cream whipped.

THE PUMPKIN HAS SET

The pie disappears from plates. Says
my reassurer,
the lady who holds the catechism,

the one whose husband's favorite was
Pumpkin Pie,
"I didn't think it would set.
But it turned out perfectly."

Stunned,
I smile my Christmas smile at her.
I have spent the last month thinking of that.
Why did she tell me she thought the custard would set,
if she didn't think it would?

Hateful.
I am a child.
We are all children. To be reassured.
I am ready to make her my enemy.

I have been duped.
Treated as a fraud
or lied to,
de-frauded.
Religion is dead: if there is no truth in the kitchen,
where could there be truth?

And I ask all of you that question,
all of you,
if there is no truth in the kitchen,
where possibly can there be truth?
                                    I expect
a betrayer in the bedroom, perhaps,
or in any other room of the house,
the helpless mechanic under the car in the garage,
the sad plumber in the bathroom.
even a hopeless fire builder or clumsy handyman.
But not the kitchen.

Women are true.
Faithful.

Honest.
Poets
speaking
committed words
through their small lives.

That was last Christmas.
I live this year
in one room,
have no kitchen,
garage,
fireplace or
bedroom.
I even share my bathroom.
Truth is lonely and unbetrayed.

I think of the motherly woman who lied, kindly, last year,
thinking
to reassure me;
wonder now at my anger,
think how easy it is to condemn,
how hard to be compassionate.

What I know is that
I have always lived alone
with my own pumpkin pie truth.

And poetry,
the reassurer,
            "Do you think it will set?"
    "Of course,
        it will be delicious."

c. 1973

The Ring

I carry it on my key chain, which itself
is a big brass ring
large enough for my wrist,
holding keys for safe-deposit box,
friends' apartments,
my house, office and faithless car.

I would like to wear it,
the only ornament on my plain body,
but it is a relic,
the husband gone to other wives,
and it could never be a symbol of sharing,
but like the gold it's made of, stands for possession, power,
the security of a throne.

So, on my key ring,
dull from resting in my dark purse,
it hangs, reminding me of failures, of beauty I once had,
of more ancient searches for an enchanted ring.

I understand, now, what that enchantment is, though.
It is being loved.
Or, conversely, loving so much that you feel loved.
And the ring hangs there
with my keys,
reminding of failure.

This vain head full of roses,
crystal,
bleeding lips,
a voice doomed to listen, forever,
to itself.

1976

The Photos

My sister in her well-tailored silk blouse hands me
the photo of my father
in naval uniform and white hat.
I say, "Oh, this is the one which Mama used to have on her
    dresser."

My sister controls her face and furtively looks at my mother,
a sad rag bag of a woman, lumpy and sagging everywhere,
like a mattress at the Salvation Army, though with no holes or
    tears,
and says, "No."

I look again,
and see that my father is wearing a wedding ring,
which he never did
when he lived with my mother. And that there is a legend on it,
"To my dearest wife,
        Love
        Chief"
And I realize the photo must have belonged to his second wife,
whom he left our mother to marry.

My mother says, with her face as still as the whole unpopulated
    part of the
state of North Dakota,
"May I see it too?"
She looks at it.

I look at my tailored sister
and my own blue-jeaned self. Have we wanted to hurt our
    mother,
sharing these pictures on this, one of the few days I ever visit or
spend with family? For her face is curiously haunted,
not now with her usual viperish bitterness,
but with something so deep it could not be spoken.

I turn away and say I must go on, as I have a dinner engagement
    with friends.
But I drive all the way to Pasadena from Whittier,
thinking of my mother's face; how I could never love her; how
    my father
could not love her either. Yet knowing I have inherited
the rag-bag body,
stony face with bulldog jaws.

I drive, thinking of that face.
Jeffers' California Medea who inspired me to poetry.
I killed my children,
but there as I am changing lanes on the freeway, necessarily
    glancing in the
rearview mirror, I see the face,
not even a ghost, but always with me, like a photo in a beloved's
    wallet.

How I hate my destiny.

1976

A Warning to the Man in Receiving at Sears

Be suspicious,
I say,
of this woman who singles you out as her favorite correspondent.
Blithely,
you load up the mails with packages,
stack boxes on your trolley at Sears,
stand at your break thinking of ice cream sundaes,
and stop off after work to visit the local framer. What, I wonder,
    do
you make of my preference for you
while reminiscing over Mr. Minimal or Rilke whose black
    mustache still
makes me faint with desire,
just to see one of my own amateurish photos.

And why do you think
just because you've stopped asking *yourself* why,
that there might not be any reason
for things you find hard to explain?

What makes you think
life is as simple as a frame house in Trenton, New Jersey,
a job in Receiving at Sears,
Saturday photographs, and fishing,
the long nights of poetry and letters?

You must think, like reflects like. Or things breed themselves.
Or even, that there is no alchemy beyond, perhaps,
baseball games and big fishing trips.

Let me tell you,
that some fish spawn up crazy streams and turn into fantastic
    things.
We have salmon and trout because they were seeded by the
    government.

In real life, things come together and create fearful combinations.
Letters do not breed letters.
Poems, poems.
Even television sets do not spawn little RCA colour sets.
No,
poets
did not make up griffins,
or hippogriffs.
Nor did we make up love, the crazy combinations
of woodworker and poet.

YES, be a
little suspicious,
I say,
not really of me. Old toothless lion.
But,
I laughed when a girl told me I was talking dangerously,
speaking of "The Special View of History," but
I know that there is danger when there is something you are not
        prepared for.
And so I say,
simply remember, like does not breed like.
You think you have a simple life.
Is it as simple as you want it?

Yes, be suspicious,
for it will be you who suddenly finds himself appalled
at how large the multiples become

even,
with one and one.

1976

How Do You Tell a Story?

The mask stares down at me,
round, open, frightened mouth, holding only three teeth,
an old grapefruit,
an old woman.
Myself,
seeing life,
as life sees me.

          When troubled with how to tell a story,
          I remind myself of Aristotle's procedure,
          Start at the beginning, my dear,
          and proceed to the middle. Conclude
          at the end, my dear. (You will never be
          the emperor of ice-cream.)
But where is the beginning?
My anger with the ironies and pain of life?
Surely, an abstraction is not a beginning?
But if the beginning begins before the story began? What then?
Well, surely, Diane, Olson was there to pave the way?
          He was brave,
          but not the emperor of ice-cream.
I will be brave, then, too.
and tell you that I am moved by two things: beauty,
and injustice.
          How *do* you tell the story of the man who
             shook
          hands?
The mask
is where I am sitting.
The story is what my mind is trying to construct.
The dialogue is what is interfering with the poem.
The poem
has not yet begun,
for a story must come first,
or there can be no poem.

299

The round, empty eyeholes,
the open mouth, as if to scream,
Where can I start,
that you will understand me? We only listen to
the very beautiful,
though sometimes the ugly man is allowed to scream at the door.

Yesterday,
sitting in a comfortable room,
a beautiful girl, with silver-blond hair to her waist,
tall, with a long oval face, her skin like expensive opals,
her lips perfect, neatly set, quietly closed,
her voice soft, her rhythms so slow
you could imagine she had been born playing the harpsichord,
she sat and told us that she was different from everyone
because she wrote poems.

Yet, every one of us in that room was a poet.
She was different only
because her body was so beautiful,
her face so serene,
her composure, so exceptional.

This beautiful moonstone of a girl
read a beautiful moonstone of a poem
in which she identified with a famous woman poet who was
        famous for being
hypersensitive and who suffered from giving poetry readings
and who, in fact, had recently died by her own automobile
        exhaust.
This pearly girl, a drink of Pernod,
accused her sensible mother of insensitivity
for, when told the story of the hypersensitive poet,
her mother replied, "Perhaps she should have had some other line
        of work
if giving readings troubled her so much."

This was considered an insensitive, even devastating thing
to have said.
                        Why do we consider "sensitivity"
                        a virtue in humans,
                        when it is the hardest stone
                        which is considered the most valuable?
                        Surely, it is the intelligence to survive,
                        not the outwitting softness
                        we should honor?

You see, I get bogged down in both narrative and comment.
For the real story of my own horror
at life,
every moment of which is almost too painful to live,
and my anger at this softness;
the truth I see,
which only allows human dignity
if you *do* carry on, if you do teach yourself to be somewhat
        gracious
under your burdens. And I think of the lady in question,
who did not, in fact, have to give poetry readings,
who was, in fact, moderately wealthy, who had,
in fact, already won many honors in that stingy world of poetry
and who could only have had one reason for doing something so
        painful to her
that it made her kill herself,
and that reason is one that I,
wearing my daily mask of horror, will never understand/ perhaps,
if you are born beautiful,
you are allowed to be
a fool?
And even win prizes for it?
While those of us
in our round-mouthed, deep-eyed masks
must survive,
because actually, no one would care
if we did not.

This story didn't really come out as I expected it to.
I haven't been able to make you understand what it is like
to love beauty,
yet be clothed in fat,
to have an ugly face,
not to be witty, athletic, or elegant,
only to have some obsession for truth and history,
to want to show things as they more completely are,
not even to be skillful,
or rich,
or even a brilliant person;
to be common,
and thus feel more different than everyone who is
lucky
or beautiful
or brilliant,
or even loved;
to be common
and thus unnoticed by all.
I want to tell you
that beauty itself
creates
injustice,
and that while everyone suffers,
only beauty is allowed any mercy
from the suffering.
I have said it before,
the ones who need love most
are the unlovable.
And how much more difficult to be ugly and sensitive and still to
    survive?

In our pain, we burrow down,
and sometimes bring out grotesque horrible beauty.
Kate said that blood is like melted rubies;
but how do you melt a ruby
without volcanic upheaval that might destroy the world?

I am screaming all of this at the door,
and you are privileged to say
it is in "bad taste."
But the simple fact is that I am an old woman who has survived
    much pain,
and I want to say to that beautiful girl,
that moonstone or opal or milky glass of Pernod,
that even if she is beautiful
she shouldn't buy fools' arguments about life.
Whether her parents understand her or not
(can parents ever understand children?)
they will love her, everyone,
even her lover
will love her, and I suppose she will say
(as did that lady poet in question) that too much love can kill
    you;

and I will only reply,
we all have to die. Better from too much love,
than none.

Better from beauty, than
the pain of none.
That mask on the wall
shows horror.
Not at life, but its perversions.
Inside,
I am shaped like a beauty,
the blood in my veins,
thank you, Kate,
is melted rubies.
It is for the upheaval of life, for persistence,
a more complex beauty,
that we twist and strain.

1975

Red Runner

She comes at me in red tights
showing satin skin underneath,
and red shorts,
a red runner's jacket,

like a bird I don't expect to see
in the rain.

Thinking of fires I have built
and how flames are not
gratuitous,
how hard it is to get even
combustible material
                    to burn,
I wonder
how
she burns
through the continuous rain

(of Juneau),
this runner, young woman,
product of the 20th century.

When I passed her,
we exchanged a rather frank
brutal
glance.

She saw
a middle-aged woman,
bundled in a coat,
walking fast on her short legs.
Probably, to this red runner,
I appeared to be some slow
sea creature,

crawling along the bottom
of the ocean.

She ran past me,
like firecrackers
(which frightened me in my youth)
or sequins glittering on a dancer's costume,
a bottle of Tabasco which had put on an Adidas,
and, irrelevantly, I think of
a Carmen Miranda movie.

But this rain has come to mean
that things don't change.
When you reach a certain age, even the flame of a
red satin-shorted runner,
coming like a can-can girl
out of the silver twilight
was not so much a change, as a proof of
sameness.
Red runner,
reminder that I live
if not
in another time,
another world,
one where a flame is not easy
to coax into life,
one where I am outdated,
or extinguished,
or under water;
certainly no location for a flame.

Tonight
with a blue sweater
her red jacket tied around her waist
red shorts again,
this time her legs naked and
white as sea scallops.

She frowned
as she passed me again.
Scorpion fish,
sea slug,
slow mover in the silvery twilight.

1978

Precision

Walking, remembering,
In the grass, I see what I think is
a small *coprinus,*
but I look more closely and decide:
> broken soda cracker.
Of course,
> this Southern California lawn
probably wouldn't be growing mushrooms.

I have already catalogued
Icelandic poppies — flamingo, salmon, vermillion,
party dresses — on the lawn,
and purple flags on another,
a whole bed of tiny white irises
and nasturtiums spilling over the cement-banked edge
of another yard.

It is March, and camellias are crowding
the bushes at every house,
pink, white, deep rose frills,
china-like,
> perfect.

Behind me, the mockingbird is singing one of his best songs,
> piccolo
> oboe
> harp
> and squeaking door all combined.
The drama is only a memory;
I arrived yesterday at the Los Angeles airport
and could not help some part of me wishing / expecting to see you,
M.,
waiting for me to return.
I suppose that is what it means
to be haunted.

In my real life
I neither expect
nor want you. Yet, some rehearsal of the past
is always with me.
Even this morning,
walking before breakfast in Santa Barbara
when I saw an ugly ranch house
with the porch light still on,
presumably from the night before,
I thought, "He hasn't come home. She is asleep
on the couch
with her clothes on, exhausted from
waiting most of the night."
And when I walked past another house
with the shades still drawn
but rock music pouring out of the closed windows, so incongruously
at 8 a.m.
thought
of a young couple who have just
awakened to make love and don't want to do it
without the right music.
And I felt safe outside in the sunshine, just observing the flowers.
There is no way I can imagine
love, sex or romance
without pain,
the cutting, cutting
sharp knife of denials;
what I want now is an orderly world
where morning is
each beautiful object in place,
the sun pouring in the window like champagne,
the china-white egg cup
with its neat boiled egg,
a burst of tulips, or poppies or
camellias on the table
                    in crystal
or cut glass,

the hot teapot, scalded and then filled with a fine dark tea,
and the day stretching plain,
unadorned
         before me,
Mozart as companion,
a book,
a book,
about death
or life
but not about
love.

We must go beyond beauty
to find it.
Invisible,
I want to wait for it
wearing the cap of darkness.

c. 1977

Silver

How much I want to sit down
at my table and pick up a heavy silver spoon to eat my soup.
    Why
do I want heavy sterling silver forks, knives, spoons, serving
    utensils? Why
do I want to put metal in my mouth?

Ask the wrong questions and you
will only get fools' answers.
Of course I do not want to put metal—even beautiful metal—in
    my mouth.
What I want
is to hold it and to somehow transform the ritual of eating
into something non-organic,
beyond the body,
beyond shit,
beyond decay,
beyond death. Of course
I want beautiful silver so that I can pretend I will never have to
    die.

c. 1976

Civilization

I admire all the brave and robust people who live on shoestrings,
somehow crafting interesting meals out of dollar bills,
drinking a passable wine for a quarter,
building houses out of old telephone poles and getting featured in
    Better Living.
They go to Europe and meet the most interesting people and
somehow earn a refund,
go to the opera in thrift store drapes and get photographed for
the society page.
Somehow, they work twenty hours a day, never sleep, have the
    most
beautiful children,
get lots of sex, write novels in their spare time, tune their own
cars,
and like Mildred Pierce bake 100 pies every day, even the day
their ten-year-old
dies of pneumonia in the hospital.

I have always been poor, and never managed well.
I took taxis when I was tired and thus had no money for food
halfway through
the week. The mediocre wines on my table cost as much as
emerald necklaces,
and I always look like I live on welfare.

I suppose this will sound like self-pity.
but I think it is only facing facts and not liking that reality.
The language of pain is difficult to transmit;
it is the glorious nature of civilization to reject suffering.

c. 1976

Searching for the Canto Fermo

For Norman Hindley

> *Moon, moon,*
> *when you leave me alone,*
> *all the darkness*
> *is an utter blackness.*
>   —Robert Creeley,
>   "A Form of Women"

Preface: Thoth, an ibis standing on one leg, or a dog-headed baboon, was given the moon, a gift created especially for him by Ra, when Thoth searched in the desert and returned to Ra his Eye, who had run away, in the form of the beautiful woman, Tefnut. His own eye, then, Thoth's the moon, that litchi nut. And Nut (noot)—that woman stretched out, her elongated body arched over the earth so that only her toes and fingertips touched her husband, Geb, the earth—Nut, Night, tall woman was befriended by Thoth, who felt sorry that Ra, jealous, decreed that Nut would not be able to bear children during any month of the year. The wily old dog-headed baboon, Thoth, he played dice with the moon, and won from him a seventy-second part of his light. Five days, on that 360-day lunar calendar, and on each of these days, respite from the rest of the year, Nut could give birth. So, she and Geb had their children after all: Isis, Osiris, Horus, Set, and Napthys. Gifts of the moon.

Norman,
the moon, like Mary-Beth's pleasing savories,
(litchi nuts stuffed with cream cheese
that has been studded with candied ginger),
unites us in our search
for communication,
that perfect word,
the measurer of time,
in Egypt (or California or Hawaii), holding a palm branch,
sometimes a silver bow
and arrows made of children's bones. Do men and women
see the same moon in the sky?

Sometimes I wonder if there is not a form of woman

which is closer to man than to that tall long-toed and -fingered
woman,
Night,
Nut,
arching over the earth like an eel,
giving birth to five hell-raising children.
Not Sapphic woman, loving other women,
but somehow that image of the cool hidden form in the rain forest
of your rescue, Norman;
the huntress with silver bow and arrow,
the goddess of chastity or virginity,
which did not mean
abstinence from sex, but rather, an unmarried woman.

The moon in that Egyptian world was a man,
a gambler,
though in so many other places
moon is woman,
but never woman of the hearth,
never woman of food and nourishing meals.
Just as the great chefs of Europe are men,
the moon was a gambling man on the Nile.

I have never been able to make myself into that wife and mother,
that woman of the hearth,
though I love to cook
and I do not make love to other women.
I have felt myself often
as that presence hidden behind the palm ferns.
I have felt myself the gambler on the Nile who felt sorry for Nut,
and let Thoth win for her a seventy-second part of my light
in order to give her babies.
I understand that giving of fertility and of sharing.
But when I have felt myself hunting, I have been terrified
at what you so calmly accepted,
shooting the mother turkey in her nest,
knowing as a woman, that turkey could be me;

oh, but what I have not felt
is some perfect combination of the word, the belly, and the hand,
and in giving birth, felt only the blood,
the pain,
the meaningless result.
When my hand reaches out to take one of those juicy litchi nuts
with ginger and cream cheese, I suddenly become
the eye, the moon, see myself in a different form,
the one you sensed in the forest,
and feel the big teeth enclosing my own form.
Norman,
the moon unites us.
I, not quite woman,
you, not quite man, with that voice singing out of you like babies
popping out of your mouth, their fat little hands holding the bow
and arrow for you,
so that you too can hide behind the ferns in the cool rain forest;

a word: that
is the huntress.
The word which is the venison you shot,
marinated in soy sauce, tequila and ginger,
the word which is fresh mangoes,
the word—white sashimi you pulled out of the ocean that
        morning,
the word in the hand-warmed glass of California cabernet.

If the moon is not spoken,
then there is no speech. Neither man nor woman invented it;
speech is what is left,
like the footprint,
after the body is gone,
what is made out of the food chewed by the big teeth,
touched by the soft lips,
the Philippine chilies arousing the throat,
all nourishment in the belly,
becomes words,

the lost five days of light
which the moon generously lost
to let Nut have her rebellious children.
Yes, Creeley, there is a form of women which will never leave
    you alone
as long as you make a word.
That word comes out of you
as you see light on the silver bow,
the glint of that moving silver arrow,
the swift death which becomes meat,

the celebration of eating, drinking, reading:
the beautiful woman with a
silver foot.

c. 1978

Breakfast

In the Spanish kingdom
of my living room:
the morning sunshine.
A polished wooden table gleams;
silence is the reflection of burnished woods/ pine,
maple, bamboo,
                  waxed to catch the yellow sun.
Outside the wall of windows,
more woods,
these turning to burgundy and gold,
russet,
scarlet,
the wind moving especially
the green leaved ones,
the branches fluttering and bowing,
my courtiers,
my trees.

The kettles boiling now —
        one with water to scald the pot,
        the second with boiling water for the tea.
This morning,
scented Earl Grey,
another courtier, this one perfumed,
a dandy, one of those too-
beautiful men I cannot resist.

On my pine and yellow canvas chair
I rest, drinking the tea,
from a white bone china cup. A remaining crumb
from last night's crusty French bread
is being dazzled on the table's surface/ now
an opal, a pearl, ivory,
a minor jewel dropped from the chest.

In the south window
four sweet basil plants have reached the
height of 18 inches each,
their lime green leaves pungent when
touched/ I give each a little clear water
and pinch off forming bud clusters.

This morning, against all rules,
an egg,
poached in water containing a few drops
of white rice-vinegar, its soft oval body
resting in a poaching cradle of tin,
on three tiny legs, its stiff upright handle
remaining cool
above the boiling white water.

Now, I turn out the egg on a plate
of translucent orange bordered with yellow and black. It
lies there with a vulnerable film over the yolk
while I take my small silver scissors & snip
four large leaves from another basil plant,
this one growing in the kitchen window.
The silver blades slice the leaves in ribbons over
the cooling egg.

Alone, at the big table
with my plate, my single
herbed egg, a goblet of
iced water with a fresh sprig of mint,
also from the kitchen window garden,
and my china cup of hot tea, I sit
down
in my morning kingdom.

Everything
we will ever have
is present

in each day's life. There is no more.
Thus, I need
this morning's royalty,
the immortality of the flesh,
the music of wood,
my perfect view of the autumn swamp.

c. 1979

Un Morceau en Forme de Poire

for Thomas Parkinson

Sitting on my kitchen table
is its yellow enamelled cast iron pot
is the remains of a liquid for poaching pears
which contains caterpillars of lemon peel
and centipede lengths of vanilla bean.
The morning kitchen has a country smell,
for my sink is stopped up,
and I couldn't wash the dishes last night
after working on my Hazelnut Chocolate Pear Torte,
and the thick porcelain jacketed top of my bain-marie has smudges
like muddy prints
over its lip, waiting for sudsy hot water and a drain
that will work.

The fragrances of vanilla and chocolate and pear mingle
with some beets and onions, waiting on the counter
for soup.
Reminding me of a moment
in my life
which perhaps was a bridge between
the girl who ate ham sandwiches on white bread with mayonnaise
    & a pickle
on Saturday evenings,
as an after-library-and-shopping treat,
and the woman who now makes Sacher Tortes,
linguine al pesto,
or stuffed vine leaves
commonly on Saturday nights.

This scene from the '50s:
       wearing the cap of darkness,
       I go to babysit for some young university faculty.
       Entering their house in the Berkeley hills, I see

plain pine floors with
threadbare Oriental carpets,
bookshelves made of boards and bricks,
hand thrown pottery.
They leave, and I hold the baby
as he cries himself to sleep.
Then I wander about the small house into the kitchen
where every dish, glass, pot or pan
seems to be dirty on the sink,
the kitchen table holding Chemex coffee pot with a bit of
amber liquid
in the bottom,
next to it, on a saucer, a paper filter full of wet grounds.
The whole kitchen was permeated
with the smell of vanilla biscuits,
and a mingle of other interesting possibilities. Some
leeks? The Viennese Roast coffee beans? Some rusks
which were also lying out?
For the first time in my life
I witnessed a soiled kitchen, used by sloppy people,
which seemed wholesome, the dirt and insects of gardens, rather
     than
neglect;
fragrant
with good food and even
a good life. Of course I spent
the evening washing the dishes
and cleaning the kitchen,
embarrassing the good-livers when they came home,
who felt required to offer me
more money.
          What a difference
between my mother's sense of good food
(baked ham and canned peas)
and this kitchen,
redolent with rosemary, lamb shoulder and garlic,

an odor I didn't know then, because I thought garlic was a stale
white powder with a slightly bitter taste.

That moment
going into the kitchen
gave me a new possibility for ORDER.
Am I destined
I wonder
to go back to the Berkeley hills someday
and live in such a house,
the messy interesting life of those young intellectuals? My own
kitchen here in the midwest has acquired
some of its jumble.

Perhaps last night
across the continent
that couple, now undoubtedly in their 60s
woke up
to a distant fragrance
of poaching pears,
a torte baking,
the ganache cream being stirred with its 15 ounces of chocolate?

Perhaps, in a dream, they saw me
as an old woman of the earth,
holding their son by the heel,
immersing him in the fire of my passionate need
trying to forge the armor of immortality
as he cried himself to sleep,
after which I went into the kitchen
and ritually cleansed it,
leaving some clarity, leaving it renewed,
and taking with me the knowledge
of common chaos,
mortal beauty,
smelling of vanilla,
an earthy bean.

1981

Making a Sacher Torte

Her hands, like albino frogs,
on the keys of a Bösendorfer,
nails short and thin like sliced almonds, fleshy fingers,
with the lightning bolt gold and diamond wedding
ring, zigzagging up to her fat knuckle,
looking out of place
on the heavy working hand.

Forty-five and fashionable,
with knit suits and suede pumps on thin-ankled feet,
short, curly blond hair and her big Jewish nose,
her husband a jeweler and she, with her rich German accent,
my piano tutor.

I, 19, and wearing home-made cotton dresses with gathered skirts,
the Niagara Falls in my eyes, no wedding, no wedding,
a girl with nothing but soapy hands and wet heart, a big
        frog-like brain;
I loved her for listening to me.
On the black piano bench, I was still the little princess whose
        golden
ball
had rolled into a well, and she,
the Frog Prince, lifted it out
with webbed hands, tossing it in the light, the gold
of her lightning bolt wedding ring catching the sun, as
        she gave me
her gold, the talk, the princess world of pianos; converting me
from Chopin who had a perfect hand, like a water lily,
to Beethoven's last work, fashioned with shovels and clubs
and the Germanic ear for long phrases, never-ending sentences,
        who
too must have had hands that looked more like
pads than the lily.

Near Christmas, she asked me one afternoon,
"Do you know what I have spent the last two days doing with
    these hands?"
(spreading them out,
heavy and short-nailed against the piano keys)
"Grinding nuts in a mortar. For a torte." And she continued to
    talk
about her culinary activities which seemed exotic then to me
and which I only recalled today after I had whirled some almonds
in my Cuisinart and was folding them into meringue for a Sacher
    Torte,
Living a life so remote from those sad Berkeley days
when I was a poor student, poor adolescent, girl from the
    working classes
where the piano bench, hard seat, was the only one I wanted;
on which I sat five hours most days,
beating my hands on the keys, out of love, as she had ground
    those nuts
by hand for her family's holiday cake.

We often talked of our favorite books and both of us were then
    avidly
reading Salinger's stories as they were published in *The New
    Yorker.*
I, wishing the Glass family were my own and she, preaching, of all
things, about how I should have more charitable feelings for my
    mother.
Yet, my own mother had none of the attributes which made Mrs.
    Ury
so compelling to me; for it was not just those hours at the piano
that made me cherish her. She was a bold and intelligent woman
    who
had forced her family to understand their danger in Germany and
    arranged
for them to leave before the disaster of the camps. She lived in a
world of books and pianos, had gone on tour all over the world,
could make her Linzer Torte without any machine. She spoke two

languages flawlessly and was generous of spirit, though a
     perfection-
ist of craft, to this provincial girl who couldn't play the piano
     very
well. She talked to me by the hour, wearing elegant clothes, and
praised me when I deserved it. Once, I remember her telling me
     about
practicing the piano in winter in Germany, when she was a
     student,
and wearing wool gloves with the finger-ends cut off, because it
     was
so cold in the studio. She gave me a sense of the meaning of sacri-
fice, and in retrospect
what I feel my own family most deprived me of was
that meaning.
That if you practiced the piano in a studio at 45 degrees in winter
it was in order to become an exceptional performer
of the world's great piano music.
That those same hands
wearing a $10,000 ring,
30 years later,
could perform the same kind of act,
as a ritual for her family,
grinding the nuts for the Christmas torte,
when, of course, her maid could
have done it
just as well.

And for me, a new meaning for the Frog Prince:
Not the lover, whose kindness made him beautiful.
That seems like a small meaning for the fairy tale.
Rather, that the transformation itself
of Frog into Prince can happen. That Mrs. Ury,
with her great frog hands, who could play with the verve of
     Rubinstein
and the delicacy of Gieseking, rescued the ball of gold
after it rolled into the well,

gave me her German self as mother,
gave me a new history, gave me
herself in marriage; for though I have not become a concert
     pianist,
I have accepted the tradition of the keyboard artists.
And her great gift to me:
to show me that impossible as it was for me to be a musician
in fact
this did not deprive me of music, but gave it back to me in more
     complex ways.

As the torte was baking in the oven, today,
I wondered idly about
how different my life would have been had Tanya Ury actually
been my mother. But of course the truth
is that she was;
how accidental is blood; how meaningless
the connection of birth. I look in the pond,
a mirror full of lilies whose long root systems curl up from the
chocolatey mud and whose green leaves might hold one of those
green music makers. In it
I see nothing but the reflection of sunlight, a golden spot
which must be projected through the thick lenses of my glasses.
As I move my face, the golden
spot dances and rolls over the water,
over the lily pads, occasionally
reflecting and glinting off one of the pale pink flower buds;
experience and memory are my real roots,
tangled, complicated, all the freeways I have traveled
to reach this moment when I lift the firm almond torte
out of the oven.

1981

Cannon Beach

One week of early morning sunshine, like a perfect rose frozen
    into an ice cube,
made us so grateful, we then loved the mist
which rolled in and blanketed us for days.
When the sun shone, we walked
the beach at dawn
while most people slept, but on the foggy mornings,
we slept too, not even hearing the horns
sounding from the rocks. Two thousand miles away,
I can only pretend to see the Pacific Ocean
no matter how early I rise.
The mist that steams up from this autumn ground
over pumpkins, the dried dinner-plate sun flowers
with bowed heads, the final red tomatoes on the browning
vines, a different beauty. It is as if everyone
in Cannon Beach is sleeping
while I'm awake, everyone, everywhere,
different from this landscape, sleeping,
only I awake, not knowing the images in each head;
as we all sleep through others' lives.

Only a few even try to imagine
what others simultaneously perceive,
and then know its futility. An act of faith
lets me believe the Pacific Ocean's still there, since I now
can't see it. That the sun exists,
though the fog entirely covers it today. That in my
sleep, I do not lose all identity, or in death
pass beyond what I now know I am.

1985

326

Removed from Natural Habitat

The feathers are thick and look sculptured,
as if they are curved, like cherries, not flat or straight.
And they grow down over the claws,
like little bedroom slippers, of fur, becoming lacy
at the ground. Also, curved
over their bills, the feathers disguise the raptor's beak,
making it protrude only like a pursed mouth
below eyes like golden coins. Part of their beauty is
in their stillness, the unblinking eyes like money that is hoarded,
the head cocked a little, the body stationary, and seemingly
unjointed.

White as new field mushrooms,
are the males; one stands there,
plump and unblemished, making me wonder what he sees, if
        anything.
The females are barred, wearing their thick
horizontal stripes as if the shadow of a prison window
had fallen on their bodies. They too
stand motionless for hours, the fringed white slippers
over their claws moving a little with the afternoon
breeze.

I too stood motionless for a long time
one afternoon, watching them,
though if my image was on the retina of even one snowy owl,
it could not have given any bird
the solace I found that day,
looking at these three creatures, placid, though totally removed
from their natural habitat.

1985

The Girls

for Margaret Atwood & Cathy Davidson

I never understood the girls
who had the sweaters
and the latest hairdos copied out of magazines
and who were not afraid of snakes.
They were the thin-hipped ones who looked good
in straight skirts, like exclamation points
behind phrases like "Wow," and "Gee Whiz."

I envied their lemon-scented hands
raised to answer asmost as many questions
as I, the ugly duckling class brain, did,
with my fat ankles,
and ass as soft as a sofa pillow.
Valerie Twadell who was Miss La Habra
at our August Corn Festival
chased me with worms.

Cathy, with her Zelda-ish bob,
and slimness that even her sorority girl students envy
tells of a snake they ritually put in the 8th grade teacher's desk;
and now you, Peggy, as I heard someone nice
call you, slender and chic as Jane Fonda,
tell of your own simple connection with snakes,
wearing them as electric tight bracelets,
wound on a willow wrist,
the delight you took in scaring others,
even men, or women like me,
who would have died had we found even a harmless little black fellow
curled in the grass.

I have never been one of the girls:
smart without being labelled with derogatory titles like

328

"the encyclopedia"
"the brain,"
graceful without watching calories,
followed by men who adored me even when I turned them away,
slow-voiced,
quiet,
with ankles like colts,
and at complete ease with snakes.
I have never been
one of the girls.
At 47, I still envy your cool acceptance
of all these gifts.
                    Some part of me
was denied
what all women have,
or are supposed to have, an ease
with the fatly coiled Python whose skin
is like milky underwear,
the thread-like green mamba who slips past
your fingers like mountain water,
the cobra who sits on the family radio
in Sri Lanka,
the cottonmouth who swims next to you all night
in muddy fertile loving water,
or the magic necklace Denise imagines around her throat.

Men see me as the Medusa,
with vipers hissing around my hair.
How ironic/ I have always been so afraid
of snakes that when I was six
I couldn't turn to the S N A K E page
in my Golden Encyclopedia.

I have never been one of the girls,
comfortable wearing a blacksnake as a belt.
Had I been Lawrence,
near his well in Sicily,

I would have turned and run. He knew
snakes were
the Lords of Life,
but I know you pretty girl women,
who handle them like hula hoops,
or jump ropes,
or pet kittens,
are the real Gods, and your ease with snakes
is proof.
In your presence I am neither man
nor woman. I am simply the one
afraid of snakes; who knows
that in this life
it is the one thing
not allowed.

1985

Braised Leeks & Framboise

for Annette Smith

The ocean
this morning
has tossed someone's garbage
over its surface,
half oranges
that make my mouth pucker for
fresh juice,
lettuce leaves
looking fragile, decorative, like scarves
for the white curling locks
of old water.
It is not hard
to think of women
coming up out of the dense green,
fully formed but not
of flesh, of some tissue, floating
goddess-like
and pale.

For breakfast
one morning
you served fresh leeks,
slender
as fingers, from a sea goddess,
braised, with butter, delicate
from the Altadena garden.

It was at your house
that I first drank
that clear heady liquor,
framboise,
an eau-de-vie, promising
that fruit did not have to be

fresh-cheeked, fat or stupid,
that it could read Proust,
or learn differential
equations.
The Saturnian taste
of old raspberries, and the moon's
clear-fingered insistence
of leek. These two intangible things
I owe you,
along with—what? or
is there more?

The image of an onion, its sweet blanket layers.
The pebbled surface
of a raspberry.

1985

Why My Mother Likes Liberace

(Liberace has many large diamond rings and impressively wears a great number of them even when he plays very difficult music)

The diamond grand,
its lid upraised,
the diamond butterfly,
the diamonds of South African mines,
clasping his fingers,
one for every tour, one ring for
his fortieth anniversary
in show business, all sitting
as if they were in howdahs, above his
fingers,
which continue to move as if
utterly
unencumbered. Not elephants but manatees
swimming in the Crystal River,
glissandos,
arpeggios, weaving hands, moving
like dragonflies
though they resemble hod-carriers
more, with the diamond-loads,
an effort of masonry.

What does it mean
never to get tired
of playing jingle bells or Chopin,
to have a chandelier
in your greenhouse,
or piano keyboard painted on the door
of one of your limousines,
to love men,
to wear silly shirts,
to have millions of pathetic old women

in love with you
    my mother:
                yr only rival with her —
    Lawrence Welk.

Why am I, the girl who gave up
the piano
to make meaning out of her life,
who never watches television,
does not own a tv set,
watching with such seriousness
this talk show
with Liberace telling about
each diamond ring he wears?
Why
thinking with admiration
of his skill, equal to most
great pianists?
              Why
am I wishing
for as much shape and purpose
from any such burden of diamonds
and tinkling keys?

Why do so many of us admire,
long for,
men who only love other men?

Do we need betrayers
and deniers
to reinforce our own failures?
Or are we searching for
some final anower,
beyond the greater measure,
beyond sex,
beyond our own mortality?

1984

What Happened

between 1850 and 1855
when Whitman lost his pretentious sense
of language and somehow got
the voice of an angel?

or between 1905 and 1915
when Stevens suddenly left Edwardian
language and found his belcanto voice?

What happened between 1963 and 1968
when Dorn left his small obscure Creeleyesque lyrics
to find the breadth to write *Gunslinger*?

It's not like flowers where one day you have
a bud, and the next day a flower. It's different,
as if one day you had a messy bag
of rotting garbage and old food, and the next
day it's transformed into fresh strawberries and cream.

What happened?

It is hopeful,
I think.

c. 1984

The Ring of Irony

What do you say to the mother
of a homosexual man
whom you once were married to,
when she asks you to return your wedding ring
because it's a family heirloom?
    "I want to keep it on my key ring
    where I carry it now,
    to remind me of loss?"
or perhaps, in spite,
    "It was the only thing
    I ever got out of the marriage.
    No. I won't give it back."
Do you say that you love irony
and have imagined your whole life
governed by understatement
and paradox?
Yet, the obvious dominates and
I ask myself,
"Why do you want to keep it?
Surely the woman deserves some comfort/
if a small piece of gold can do it,
who can object?"
Wallowing again, in the obvious,
I wonder at my meanness,
my own petty anger
at men who love other men,
alas, some of them are/ have been
my best friends. Irony?
No. The obvious.
Why do you want that circle of gold
lying in your purse with keys
and checkbooks? I nudge myself.
Why don't you purchase an ounce of gold
and carry it in a velvet bag instead. Your
own.

Worth so much more.
Of course. The obvious.
Because the other was given,
not bought, and you
have never asked the return of your gifts, but
you know, Diane, why
you anguish over putting the ring in the box and
mailing it off to
Corona, California.
So obvious.
Because you believe in the gifts
freely given
to appease destiny.
You too would sacrifice
Iphigenia or Isaac
for the cap of darkness,
having given your children
for poetry,
having given your sexuality
for beautiful men,
having relinquished honor
for music.
The circle of gold,
that ring, symbolizes
the pact.
To give it back says the giving was meaningless.
Fate does not honor your bargain,
Ms. Wakoski. Not irony,
the obvious:
you have no husband,
          no house,
          no children,
          no country.
You have no fame,
          fortune,
only remaindered books,
and innocent students who

337

stab you
with their lack of understanding,
asking, no not ironically,
"Did you give a lot of readings
when you were young?"
Finally, the understatement, the irony, when I say,
"yes," and the past swallows up everything,
leaving the obvious,
and now that handsome woman in California
wants to take the ring.

Soap opera of the middle-aged
mid-Western
schoolteacher?
What do you say when irony deserts you
for the maudlin obvious?
"I am mailing you the ring.
Your claim is greater than mine."

Irony? No, the obvious.

c. 1982

Joyce Carol Oates Plays the Saturn Piano

for Joyce Carol Oates who, several years
ago, began to study the piano again

I promised myself
that if, by 40, I had won a Pulitzer Prize for Poetry
I would let myself play the piano again.
This was when I was 20,
still pounding on the keyboard,
relentlessly, as if I were chopping down dozens of trees,
and splitting the logs,
making enough firewood for a castle
to be heated throughout an entire Russian winter.

I longed for tea in Samovars,
and to wear sable.
The Snow Queen glinted snow roses, ice violets, tuna-bright
    daggers,
as I spoke with stiff lips.
My fingers were frozen too,
against the brilliance of local pianists
        Abromovitch,
        del Tredici,
        Goodman,
        Ury.
Unlike you,
during the four undergraduate years,
I did not win a Phi Beta Kappa key,
write three novels and marry my sweetheart. I ran across
Dwinelle Plaza barefooted in winter
carrying a wicker birdcage,
I wept in classes, puffed up like a mushroom,
spoke laments
which embarrassed everyone,
and played, played, played,

Beethoven and
Chopin
mostly, trying to substitute music
for sex, for love, for security and kindness.
Unlike you,
I was no combination,
clicking shut like an expensive lock,
of beauty and brains.
I did not have your dark eyes like Godiva chocolates
or your Emily Brontë smile.
I could not even talk,
though most poets' lips moved like a swarm of Japanese fantailed
goldfish at feeding, pursing for the scattered breadcrumbs.

It was California, but my lips were rigid
with some Northern climate
outside of geography.
My fingers too, though I flexed and flexed
them.
How I hated the rich girls in my classes
who were being
expensively
psychoanalysed (how I needed to tell
my histories),
and who played Bach
sitting decorously, neatly, on the piano bench
like little hair brushes,
while I grimaced and swayed and rocked on the bench
with each cadence, until my practice room
must have seemed like
an exercise cell for some crippled gymnast,
one who had to do all her exercises sitting
in a single position.

The first years of not playing
were empty ones.
Perhaps I was grateful not to own a stereo, have records or afford

many concerts.
From Cage and Creeley I learned about silence.
About the "missing"
as part of the object.
And the possibilities I longed for
bred in this silence.
The Ice Queen showed me the beauty of death,
and longing.
The ice needle words which I could emit
from frozen mouth.
Each decade
I would look at my hands,
losing their muscles and flexibility,
until after 20 years
I realized that I could no more return to playing the piano
with any of the skill I'd worked for
than one could go out on a winter day and pick a favorite
rose
which he had seen bloom months ago
and remembered,
from that summer. Not even the dried hip
would be there.

And I have passed 40 now,
some years ago.
No Pulitzer Prize.
You have had numerous awards with that big one looming up
for you now, very soon,
while my name is never even mentioned in connection
with such things.

And I thought I had forgotten all about that young pledge
until I entered your house
and saw the upright piano covered
with music I used to play,
and heard your voice,

flashing like a marlin when it jumps and twists in Caribbean
        waters,
saying, "Yes I am
taking piano lessons again. I practice
two hours every day."

Envy?
No. Past that.
A sense of failure?
Perhaps. For I gave up something
I loved/ to attain something
unknown, and now I have neither.

What do I have?

I wear the rings of Saturn, all
nine of them on my hands,
and when I listen to the keyboard
I hear a music
beyond what anyone can play.

All that wood I chopped
years ago
makes a bright fire,
and when it is dead,
maybe the cinders will begin to move in orbit,
begin whirling,
begin spinning,
around me. I will be Saturn,
and my rings will be
hundreds of pianos, rotating,
revolving around my dried ashy body.

When you play your piano, Joyce,
a chunk of rock might fall into your garden, near the river,
where an old pike nuzzles down near its industrial bottom.
You will say,

"I am playing Saturn's piano,"
and the ring on your long-married, sweetheart, wonderful
    prize-winning
finger will, perhaps, for a moment
glow, as will the rock in your garden,
as a piano always does
when someone with inspired hands throws it into orbit.

1982

Printed September 1988 in Santa Barbara & Ann
Arbor for the Black Sparrow Press by Graham
Mackintosh & Edwards Brothers Inc. Design by
Barbara Martin. This edition is published in
paper wrappers; there are 400 hardcover trade
copies; 200 hardcover copies have been numbered
& signed by the author; & 50 numbered copies
with an original holograph poem have been
handbound in boards by Earle Gray & are signed
by the author.

Photo: Robert Turney

DIANE WAKOSKI was born in Whittier, California in 1937 and educated at U.C., Berkeley. She has published sixteen collections of poems, and many other slim volumes. Her two most recent collections of poems from Black Sparrow were *The Collected Greed, Parts 1-13* (1984) and *The Rings of Saturn* (1986). The University of Michigan Press published her criticism in *Toward a New Poetry* (1980). She is currently Writer in Residence at Michigan State University.

28 Days

DATE DUE

WITHDRAWN

GAYLORD

PRINTED IN U.S.A.